MCSA Windows Server 2016 Certification Guide: Exam 70-741

The ultimate guide to becoming MCSA certified

Sasha Kranjac
Vladimir Stefanovic

BIRMINGHAM - MUMBAI

MCSA Windows Server 2016 Certification Guide: Exam 70-741

Commissioning Editor: Gebin George
Acquisition Editor: Shrilekha Inani
Content Development Editor: Abhishek Jadhav
Technical Editor: Pratik Shet
Copy Editor: Safis Editing
Language Support Editor: Mary McGowan
Project Coordinator: Jagdish Prabhu
Proofreader: Safis Editing
Indexer: Rekha Nair
Graphics: Alishon Mendonsa
Production Coordinator: Jisha Chirayil

First published: April 2019

Production reference: 1300419

Published by Packt Publishing Ltd.
Livery Place
35 Livery Street
Birmingham
B3 2PB, UK.

ISBN 978-1-78953-560-0

www.packtpub.com

`mapt.io`

Mapt is an online digital library that gives you full access to over 5,000 books and videos, as well as industry leading tools to help you plan your personal development and advance your career. For more information, please visit our website.

Why subscribe?

- Spend less time learning and more time coding with practical eBooks and Videos from over 4,000 industry professionals

- Improve your learning with Skill Plans built especially for you

- Get a free eBook or video every month

- Mapt is fully searchable

- Copy and paste, print, and bookmark content

Packt.com

Did you know that Packt offers eBook versions of every book published, with PDF and ePub files available? You can upgrade to the eBook version at `www.packt.com` and as a print book customer, you are entitled to a discount on the eBook copy. Get in touch with us at `customercare@packtpub.com` for more details.

At `www.packt.com`, you can also read a collection of free technical articles, sign up for a range of free newsletters, and receive exclusive discounts and offers on Packt books and eBooks.

Contributors

About the authors

Sasha Kranjac is a security and Azure expert and instructor with more than two decades of experience in the field. He began programming in Assembler on Sir Clive Sinclair's ZX, met Windows NT 3.5 and the love exists since. Sasha owns an IT Training and Consulting company and helps companies and individuals to embrace the cloud and be safe in the cyberspace. He is a Microsoft MVP, Microsoft Certified Trainer (MCT), MCT Regional Lead, Certified EC-Council Instructor (CEI) and currently holds more than 60 technical certifications. Sasha is a frequent speaker at various international conferences and consultant and trainer for some of the largest Fortune 500 companies.

Vladimir Stefanovic is Microsoft Certified Trainer (MCT) and System Engineer with 10+ years of experience in IT industry. Over the IT career, Vladimir has worked in all areas of IT administration, from IT technician to current System Engineer position. As a lead System Engineer in Serbian IT company SuperAdmins and lead technician trainer in Admin Training Center, he successfully delivered a numerous of project and courses. He is also active conference speaker, with a long list of conferences like as MCT Summits (USA, Germany, Greece), ATD, WinDays, KulenDayz, Sinergija (Regional Conferences). He is a leader of a few user groups and active community member, with mission to share knowledge as much as possible.

About the reviewer

Mustafa Toroman is Program Architect and Senior System Engineer with Authority Partners. With years of experience in designing and monitoring infrastructure solutions, lately most focused on designing new solutions in the cloud and migrating existing solutions to the cloud. He is very interested in DevOps processes and he's also Infrastructure as Code enthusiast. Mustafa has over 30 Microsoft certificates and has been Microsoft Certified Trainer for last 6 years. Often speaks on international conferences (about cloud technologies and has been awarded MVP for Microsoft Azure last three years in a row. Mustafa also authored *Hands-On Cloud Administration in Azure* and co-authored *Learn Node.JS with Azure*, both published by Packt.

Packt is searching for authors like you

If you're interested in becoming an author for Packt, please visit `authors.packtpub.com` and apply today. We have worked with thousands of developers and tech professionals, just like you, to help them share their insight with the global tech community. You can make a general application, apply for a specific hot topic that we are recruiting an author for, or submit your own idea.

Table of Contents

Preface

MCSA: Windows Server 2016 is one of the most sought-after certifications for IT professionals, which includes working with Windows Server and performing administrative tasks in it. It targets Exam 70-740, Exam 70-741, Exam 70-742, and Exam 70-743 certifications, and the demand for these certifications is increasingly high.

This book will start with installing, upgrading, and migrating to Windows Server 2016, and will cover imaging and deployment, going on to cover high availability and clustering. Then, we will deep dive into fundamental concepts such as core networking, DNS, DHCP, and storage, proceeding on to Hyper-V, network access, and Distributed File System. It will also explain advanced networking topics such as software-defined networking and high-performance networking. Furthermore, it will also cover advanced identity topics in Windows Server 2016, such as Active Directory installation and configuration, Group Policy, Active Directory Certificate Services, and Active Directory Federation Services and Rights Management. Toward the end of this book, test questions and mock preparation items will help you to prepare for the certification.

By the end of this book, you will be able to complete MCSA: Windows Server 2016 certification with more confidence.

Who this book is for

This book is targeted toward system administrators or Windows Server administrators who are interested in passing the MCSA certification with ease.

What this book covers

Chapter 1, *Configuring Core Networking*, explains IPv4 and IPv6 addressing, interoperability, and routing. Before any operating system can talk to its siblings, it needs to have an address—like you do (well, like houses do) to be able to receive post. Correctly configured network addresses are fundamental to rock-solid networking functions and services that build upon them, such as DNS, DHCP, and Active Directory.

Chapter 2, *Configuring DNS*, explains DNS installation requirements and proceeds on to more advanced topics necessary for DNS to function correctly: the configuration of root hints, forwarders and DNS policies, and the configuration and management of zones and records. Having implemented IP addressing correctly, in this chapter, we can proceed with the installation of the DNS server role.

Chapter 3, *Configuring DHCP*, explains how to install and configure the DHCP server role, how to create and configure scopes and policies, how to back up and restore a DHCP server, and how to achieve high availability. Parallel to the IP addressing topic, more complex environments need to have the possibility to configure IP addresses automatically. This chapter introduces the Dynamic Host Configuration Protocol, or DHCP—a service in Windows Server 2016 that handles IP addresses.

Chapter 4, *Understanding IPAM*, introduces IPAM provisioning, configuring the discovery of infrastructure servers, and configuration. For the most complex environments, consisting of multiple DHCP and DNS servers, there is the IP Address Management or IPAM role in Windows Server 2016. This chapter explains IPAM management, administration, and auditing.

Chapter 5, *Implementing Network Access*, talks about the Remote Access Service (RAS) role with Virtual Private Network (VPN) site-to-site solutions, showing different VPN protocol options and authentication possibilities. To connect to multiple sites or branch offices, we need a secure and reliable connection. Windows Server 2016 has powerful connectivity options and network access technologies. This chapter shows how to use DirectAccess to enable connectivity without the need for traditional VPN connections. At the end of the chapter, we'll explain the role of Network Policy Server (NPS) as a way to provide centralized authentication and authorization.

Chapter 6, *Understanding Distributed File System*, briefly explains file service basics and then proceeds on to the installation and configuration of Distributed File System, a technology that enables the grouping of shared network folders. The installation and configuration of DFS are the basics that enable DFS replication, and in this chapter, we will find out how to configure DFS namespaces and replication settings and understand DFS replication. Additionally, we will configure BranchCache, a bandwidth optimization technology designed to work over wide area networks.

Chapter 7, *Advanced Networking Infrastructure*, introduces and explains the term software-defined networking (SDN). SDN is a term that refers to data center virtualization, where compute, storage, and networking layers are virtualized. To be able to achieve maximum networking performance and reliability, Windows Server 2016 has numerous technologies, and in this chapter, we'll explain how they work and how to configure them correctly, covering scenarios and requirements for SDN in Windows Server 2018.

To get the most out of this book

Before you start with this book with a view to preparing for Exam 70-741, you should have an understanding of networking in Windows Server 2016, virtualization, and related services. Experience of configuring Windows Server 2012 and Windows Server 2016, as well as working with virtualization, is required to better understand storage and virtualization-related services. The following Windows Server roles and services will be used in this book:

- DNS
- DHCP
- IPAM
- DFS

Download the color images

We also provide a PDF file that has color images of the screenshots/diagrams used in this book. You can download it here: https://www.packtpub.com/sites/default/files/downloads/9781789535600_ColorImages.pdf.

Conventions used

There are a number of text conventions used throughout this book.

CodeInText: Indicates code words in text, database table names, folder names, filenames, file extensions, pathnames, dummy URLs, user input, and Twitter handles. Here is an example: "To configure Teredo, use the PowerShell Set-NetTeredoConfiguration cmdlet."

A block of code is set as follows:

```
0011110110101111 0010000000001011 0000000000000100 0011110011110010
0100000011111110 0000000000000000 0101000011111110 1111111110101011
```

Any command-line input or output is written as follows:

```
$Sample_RoutingDomain = "SampleTenant"
Install-RemoteAccess -MultiTenancy
Enable-RemoteAccessRoutingDomain -Name $Sample_RoutingDomain -Type All -
PassThru
```

Bold: Indicates a new term, an important word, or words that you see onscreen. For example, words in menus or dialog boxes appear in the text like this. Here is an example: "Select **RIP Version 2 for Internet Protocol** and click **OK.**"

 Warnings or important notes appear like this.

 Tips and tricks appear like this.

Get in touch

Feedback from our readers is always welcome.

General feedback: If you have questions about any aspect of this book, mention the book title in the subject of your message and email us at customercare@packtpub.com.

Errata: Although we have taken every care to ensure the accuracy of our content, mistakes do happen. If you have found a mistake in this book, we would be grateful if you would report this to us. Please visit www.packt.com/submit-errata, selecting your book, clicking on the Errata Submission Form link, and entering the details.

Piracy: If you come across any illegal copies of our works in any form on the Internet, we would be grateful if you would provide us with the location address or website name. Please contact us at copyright@packt.com with a link to the material.

If you are interested in becoming an author: If there is a topic that you have expertise in and you are interested in either writing or contributing to a book, please visit authors.packtpub.com.

Reviews

Please leave a review. Once you have read and used this book, why not leave a review on the site that you purchased it from? Potential readers can then see and use your unbiased opinion to make purchase decisions, we at Packt can understand what you think about our products, and our authors can see your feedback on their book. Thank you!

For more information about Packt, please visit packt.com.

Configuring Core Networking 1

Before any operating system can "talk" to its siblings, it needs to have an address – in that same way that you do (well, houses do) in order to be able to receive post. Correctly configured network addresses are fundamental to rock-solid networking functions and services that build on, such as **Domain Name System (DNS)**, **Dynamic Host Configuration Protocol (DHCP)**, and Active Directory.

This chapter explains IPv4 and IPv6 addressing, interoperability, and routing in the Windows Server 2016 operating system.

In this chapter, we will cover the following topics:

- Configuring IPv4 addresses and options
- **Classless Inter-Domain Routing (CIDR)**
- Subnetting
- Configuring IPv6 addressing
- IPv4 and IPv6 interoperability
- Configuring routing

Technical requirements

In this chapter, you will need the Windows Server 2016 operating system – either the Standard Edition or the Enterprise Edition. If you plan to use your own lab to prepare for the exam, then you can use Hyper-V on Windows Server or the Windows client operating systems. Of course, you can practice on real hardware as well, but it is a lot more practical to practice in a virtualized environment. Any virtualization environment or hypervisor will work just fine, and you can set up your own practice lab in the Microsoft Azure cloud as well.

Configuring addressing

At the heart of every networked, connected system, whether hardware or software, there needs to be a solid, stable network foundation, which is backed up by a properly working addressing scheme. Only then can you build reliable core and advanced services on top of it. Windows Server 2016 is no exception and many core roles and features are directly dependable on the fundamental networking services. These roles and capabilities are instrumental in network presence and server functionality, such as DHCP, DNS, **Active Directory Domain Services (AD DS)**, **Network Policy Server (NPS)**, or **Internet Information Server (IIS)**.

Configuring IPv4 addresses and options

Microsoft Windows uses a collection of protocols to communicate over the network, called **Transmission Control Protocol/Internet Protocol (TCP/IP)**. TCP/IP is a suite of protocols developed in 1969 by the U.S. Department of Defense in order to connect different branches of the U.S. military and enable them to communicate. At first, in the early 1960s, different U.S. military departments chose different vendors as computer system suppliers. For instance, the navy chose Unisys, the army chose **Digital Equipment Corporation (DEC)**, and the air force chose **International Business Machines (IBM)**. After a while, the departments needed to communicate between themselves and to exchange data, but it was difficult since each department had a different computer system. The Department of Defense started a project to connect all the branches and enable them to communicate. The TCP/IP suite of protocols was developed, and the fourth iteration of the IP protocol, IPv4, became the standard to connect the world's computers and devices.

TCP provides the reliable delivery of messages and defines delivery mechanisms for data transfers. In comparison, IP manages network routing from the sender to the receiver. The TCP/IP suite of protocols works by mapping to a layered protocol architecture stack, or model, and it is aligned with the **Open System Interconnect (OSI)** architectural model. The OSI uses a seven-layer architecture model, while TCP/IP uses a four-layer architectural model. Additionally, each TCP/IP layer corresponds to one or more OSI layers.

The four layers that the TCP/IP model uses are network interface, internet, transport, and application. The seven OSI layers are physical, data-link, network, transport, session, presentation, and application.

The following diagram shows the TCP/IP protocol architecture layers along with the OSI model layers:

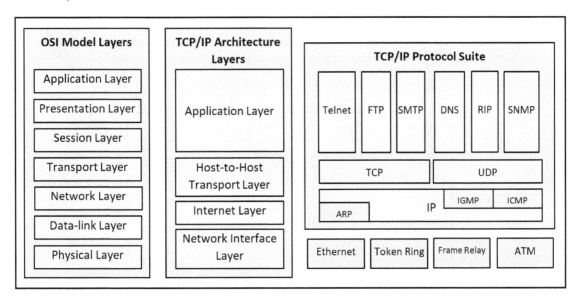

Each layer provides specific functionality within its architectural layer model, such as routing, addressing, packaging, or session communication. There are four **TCP/IP Architecture Layers**, as shown in the diagram: **Network Interface Layer**, **Internet Layer**, **Host-to-Host** or **Transport Layer**, and **Application Layer**.

The network interface layer or network access layer addresses physical transmissions, by putting packets of data onto the medium and retrieving data packets off the medium.

The internet layer deals with routing, addressing, and packaging tasks; the common internet protocols are **IP**, **Address Resolution Protocol (ARP)**, **Internet Group Management Protocol (IGMP)**, and the **Internet Control Message Protocol (ICMP)**.

The transport layer protocols are TCP and the **User Datagram Protocol (UDP)**. TCP is a reliable, connection-oriented protocol, which is responsible for packet delivery, while UDP is a connectionless and unreliable protocol, which is used to transfer smaller-sized packets.

The application layer is the protocol that directly communicates and exchanges data with applications; the best-known representatives are **Hypertext Transfer Protocol (HTTP)**, **File Transfer Protocol (FTP)**, and **Simple Mail Transfer Protocol (SMTP)**.

TCP also uses ports, which are specific endpoints for data packet delivery. Let's suppose that a user is browsing the internet using a web browser, sending and receiving emails through their favorite email client, and uploading a file using an FTP client. *If there were no ports, how would the computer know what data packet belongs to each application?* The answer is by using standardized and predefined port numbers. This is so that multiple applications can send and receive information to and from the network at the same time.

The following screenshot lists some well-known ports:

Protocol	Port	Function
HTTP	80	Web
HTTPS	443	Web (Secure)
FTP	20, 21	File transfer
SFTP	22	File transfer (Secure)
FTPS	989, 990	File transfer (Secure)
SIP	5060	VoIP (Internet phone)
DNS	53	Name resolution
SMTP	25	Mail
POP3	110	POP mailbox
IMAP	143	IMAP mailbox
Telnet	23	Remote login
SSH	122	Remote login (Secure)
NNTP	119	Usenet
NNTPS	563	Usenet (Secure)
IRC	194	Chat
NTP	123	Network time
SNMP	161, 162	Network management
Kerberos	88	Authentication

IP address

In order to communicate, TCP/IP ensures that each host on the network has its own logical IP address. There is also a physical, or a **Media Access Control** (**MAC**), address that represents physical communication hardware, which is used to send and receive data packets. The host IP address is a 32-bit binary number in a binary notation, known also as **dotted decimal notation**. Such a number, comprised of 32 "zeros" or "ones", is hard to read and, therefore, is segmented into four parts, called **octets**. Such a notation is also called the **w.x.y.z** notation:

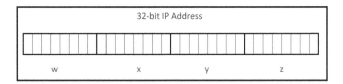

Binary numbers use the number two (2) as the base for calculations and use only two characters to form a number—that is, zero (0) and one (1). The low-order bit or the rightmost bit has a decimal value of one (1) and the leftmost or high-order bit has the decimal value of 128. If the value of the bit in an octet is set to zero (0), then the value of the bit is multiplied by zero, and the result is, naturally, zero. If the value of the bit in an octet is set to one (1), then the value of the bit is multiplied by one, and the result of the multiplication is the actual value of the bit. The sum of all multiplied values is the decimal value of the octet.

For example, the `10101000` binary number is calculated as follows:

```
1×128 + 0×64 + 1×32 + 0×16 + 1×8 + 0×4 + 0×2 + 0×1 =
= 128 + 0 + 32 + 0 + 8 + 0 + 0 + 0 = 168
```

The following diagram demonstrates the relationship and conversion from a binary to a decimal notation:

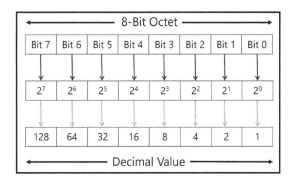

The following example shows an IPv4 number in binary format. As you can see, reading, interpreting, and performing calculations with numbers displayed in this format is very hard:

```
32-bit number: 11000000101010000000000100001100
```

To enhance readability, a number is separated into octets, however, even so, calculating values is not easy:

```
11000000 10101000 00000001 00001100
```

Each binary octet is then converted to a decimal number:

	w	x	y	z
Binary format	11000000	10101000	00000001	00001100
Decimal number	192	168	1	12

Each octet or decimal is separated by a period or a dot, and is displayed in dotted decimal notation for better readability: **192.168.1.12**. In this way, the hardly-readable binary format that machines use is presented in a form that we can understand better.

IPv4 has three types of addresses, as follows:

- **Broadcast**: This type of address is used in "one-to-everyone" communications and is assigned to all network interfaces on a subnet. Packets sent from an interface to a broadcast address receive all the interfaces on that network.
- **Multicast**: This type of address is used in "one-to-many" types of communication, where a sender transmits a packet that receives more than one network interface.
- **Unicast**: This type of address is used in "one-to-one" communications, where one network interface sends the data packet and only one network interface receives the packet.

Unicast addresses are also defined by a network ID and a host ID. The network ID, network address, or a subnet is a fixed portion of an IPv4 address that groups a set of network interfaces located on the same network segment. Routers separate network segments that must be unique on a TCP/IP network. A host ID or a host address represents a variable part of an IPv4 address and is unique to the network subnet.

Internet address classes

Internet address classes are defined to segment the available address space into networks of different sizes. Classes A, B, and C are reserved for unicast communication, D is reserved for multicast addresses, and the E class is reserved for experimental uses. The addressing scheme where classes are used is called classful.

Furthermore, the term **subnet mask** describes which bits of an address define the network ID, and which bits represent the host ID.

The following table presents the default subnet masks and address classes:

Address Class	Network (n) and Host (h) address octet layout	Default subnet mask	Number of networks	Number of hosts
Class A	n.h.h.h	255.0.0.0	128	16,777,216
Class B	n.n.h.h	255.255.0.0.	16,384	65,536
Class C	n.n.n.h	255.255.255.0	2,097,152	256

The class A address range

The class A network has the high-order bit set to zero. It includes address ranges from `0.0.0.0` to `128.0.0.0`. It has an 8-bit prefix for network IDs (`/8`) and a subnet mask that is equivalent to `255.0.0.0`. The `0.0.0.0` network is reserved for special purposes and `127.0.0.0` is reserved as a loopback address range, which leaves 126 out of 128 possible network IDs for use. The reservation of a whole `127.0.0.0` network ID for a loopback address is an obvious example of extremely bad address assignment planning. This bad planning originated in the early days of the internet; back then, we could not imagine how big and important the internet would become and how the explosion of interconnected devices would lead to the depletion of the IPv4 address space. The class A has 128 network IDs and 16,777,216 possible host addresses.

The following screenshot shows the structure of a class A address:

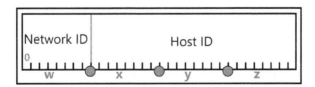

The class B address range

The class B network has two high-order bits set to 10, includes ranges from `128.0.0.0` to `192.0.0.0`, has a 16-bit prefix for network IDs (`/16`), and has a subnet mask that is equivalent to `255.255.0.0`. Class B has a maximum of 16,384 network IDs and 65,536 possible host addresses.

The following screenshot shows the structure of a class B address:

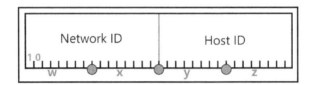

The class C address range

The class C network has 2 high-order bits set to 110, includes ranges from `192.0.0.0` to `224.0.0.0`, has a 24-bit prefix for network IDs (`/24`), and has a subnet mask that is equivalent to `255.255.255.0`. Class C has the biggest number of possible network IDs or 2,097,152 network addresses, with each network capable of addressing 256 hosts.

The following screenshot shows the structure of a class C address:

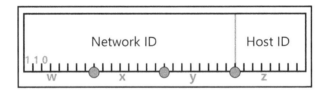

The class D address range

Class D is exclusively reserved for IPv4 multicast addresses. Here, the high-order bits are set to 1,110 and network addresses range from `224.0.0.0` to `240.0.0.0`.

The class E address range

Class E is reserved for experimental use, where the high-order bits are set to 1,111 and the class uses the network ID of `240.0.0.0`.

Understanding CIDR

Network classes were designed with then-current situations in mind, where class A was designed to have the smallest number of networks but the largest number of hosts per network, and class C was designed to have the largest number of networks but the smallest number of hosts per network. The class A networks were distributed among the largest corporations that were supposed to have the largest number of hosts, and the class C networks were supposed to be distributed to the various companies that were smaller in size.

In classless addressing, the addresses no longer belong to class A, B, or C – as the name implies – but the suffix to the address is added. This defines how many high-order bits of the address belong to the network ID and how many belong to the host ID; this is also called CIDR.

For example, a `192.168.1.12` address is a class C address. However, in a CIDR notation, this address is noted as `192.168.1.12/24` if a default, class-specific subnet mask is used. In this case, `/24` means that the 24 high-order bits are used for the network ID portion and the remaining 8 bits are used for the host ID portion:

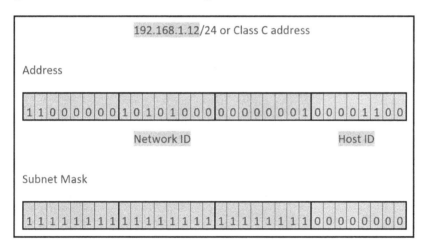

The **Internet Assigned Numbers Authority (IANA)** is the authoritative body that assigns or issues the blocks of CIDR addresses to regional internet registries. For example, the body is responsible for addressing assignments to European, Asian, or North American internet registries, which then further assign the blocks of addresses to local internet registrars. By using classless addressing, finer and adjustable segmentation of the address space is possible, resulting in fewer addresses being wasted.

In a usual network addressing scheme, the number of addresses available for assignment to hosts is *n-2*, where *n* is the maximum number of available network IDs in a network. For example, there are 256 host IDs in a class C 192.168.1.0 network. The number of addresses that can be assigned to hosts is 256 - 2 = 254. The first host address (192.168.1.0, in this example) is always reserved for referring to the network itself and the last network ID (192.168.1.255, in this example) is always reserved to a broadcast address.

In more complex network environments, less common addressing schemes are possible, such as networks with a /31 and /32 suffix. These are one-host networks, where the host ID is equal to the broadcast address. However, these are beyond the scope of this book and won't be mentioned further.

The following table shows the values of IPv4 CIDR block prefixes, available addresses, and subnet masks:

CIDR block address format	Subnet mask	Number of hosts/nodes
/32	255.255.255.255	1
/31	255.255.255.254	2
/30	255.255.255.252	4
/29	255.255.255.248	8
/28	255.255.255.240	16
/27	255.255.255.224	32
/26	255.255.255.192	64
/25	255.255.255.128	128
/24	255.255.255.0	256
/23	255.255.254.0	512
/22	255.255.252.0	1,024
/21	255.255.248.0	2,048
/20	255.255.240.0	4,096
/19	255.255.224.0	8,192
/18	255.255.192.0	16,384
/17	255.255.128.0	32,768
/16	255.255.0.0	65,536
/15	255.254.0.0	131,072
/14	255.252.0.0	262,144
/13	255.248.0.0	524,288
/12	255.240.0.0	1,048,576
/11	255.224.0.0	2,097,152
/10	255.192.0.0	4,194,304
/9	255.128.0.0	8,388,608
/8	255.0.0.0	16,777,216
/7	254.0.0.0	33,554,432
/6	252.0.0.0	67,108,864
/5	248.0.0.0	134,217,728
/4	240.0.0.0	268,435,456
/3	224.0.0.0	536,870,912
/2	192.0.0.0	1,073,741,824
/1	128.0.0.0	2,147,483,648
/0	0.0.0.0	4,294,967,296

In the next section, we will learn how to divide a network range into smaller, multiple networks.

Subnetting

Subnetting is a technique to divide a network (a subnet ID or a network range) into several, smaller networks. In other words, subnetting is a method to divide a network range into smaller, multiple networks by "borrowing" the host ID bits and turning them into network ID bits. Let's suppose that a network registrar authority, or an **internet service provider** (**ISP**), has assigned you a block of addresses. Or, that the current, internal, networking scheme in your company allows you to use a certain network ID. The network in this example is a class C network, `192.168.0.0`, with a subnet mask of `255.255.255.0` and a suffix network of `/24`:

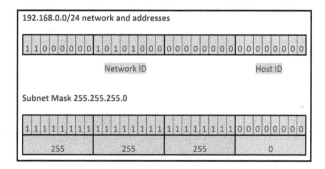

This configuration gives you only one network with 254 (256-2) addressable host addresses.

In order to be able to accommodate more networks within a given range, you need to subnet the network. If, for example, you need seven networks, then you need to take the number of bits assigned to a host ID portion and assign them to a network ID part of the network.

So, how many bits should you take? The answer is the number of bits that will give you enough network IDs. The simple calculation of *2n*, where *n* is the number of bits you take, will give you the number of available networks. In this case, since you need 7 networks, the calculation of 23 (that is, borrowing 3 bits) will give you a number of 8, which is slightly above your requirements and satisfies the required number of networks. The downside, however, is that subnetting increases the number of networks but decreases the number of hosts (or host IDs). This is logical, because while you have more bits that represent the network ID, you also have fewer bits available for the host ID portion.

So, how do you or the computer know which bits you have borrowed from the host ID portion? Well, the subnet mask provides this information. The subnetting process also involves changing or increasing the subnet mask to the appropriate value that determines which bits are used for the network ID and which are used for the host ID. The following example shows you which bits have been "borrowed", which part is the network ID, and which part is the host ID:

192.168.0.0/27 network and addresses

| 1 1 0 0 0 0 0 0 | 1 0 1 0 1 0 0 0 | 0 0 0 0 0 0 0 0 | 0 0 0 0 0 0 0 0 |

Network ID   Host ID

Subnet Mask 255.255.255.192

1 1 1 1 1 1 1 1	1 1 1 1 1 1 1 1	1 1 1 1 1 1 1 1	1 1 1 0 0 0 0 0
Network		Subnet	Host ID
255	255	255	192

This subnet configuration allows you to have 23=8 networks and 25-2=30 hosts in total. Depending on the number of networks/hosts you need, you can increase or decrease the number of subnet bits (or borrowed bits) to adjust the number of hosts and networks. The following table shows the number of subnets needed and the number of bits to borrow up to the 16 subnet bits. You can easily calculate the number of available subnets all the way to the theoretically borrowed 32 bits if you are subnetting a class A network range:

Number of Subnets needed	Number of Subnet or Host Bits to "borrow"
1-2	1
3-4	2
5-8	3
9-16	4
17-32	5
33-64	6
65-128	7
129-256	8
257-512	9
513-1,024	10
1,025-2,048	11
2,049-4,096	12
4,097-8,192	13
8,193-16,384	14
16,385-32,768	15
32,769-65,536	16

As mentioned earlier, the network ID portion of an address (where the host ID bits are set to zero) represents a network ID, and the last host ID (where all the host ID bits are set to one) represents a broadcast address. The following table shows the subnetted `192.168.0.0/27` network range with all its corresponding network IDs:

Subnet	Binary Representation	Subnet Address Prefix
1	11000000.10101000.00000000.**000**00000	192.168.0.0/27
2	11000000.10101000.00000000 **001**00000	192.168.0.32/27
3	11000000.10101000.00000000.**010**00000	192.168.0.64/27
4	11000000.10101000.00000000.**011**00000	192.168.0.96/27
5	11000000.10101000.00000000.**100**00000	192.168.0.128/27
6	11000000.10101000.00000000.**101**00000	192.168.0.160/27
7	11000000.10101000.00000000.**110**00000	192.168.0.192/27
8	11000000.10101000.00000000.**111**00000	192.168.0.224/27

After subnetting `192.168.0.0/24` to `192.168.0.0/27`, the available subnet network IDs, host ID address ranges, and broadcast addresses will be as follows:

Subnet	Network ID	First Host ID	Last Host ID	Broadcast address
1	192.168.0.0/27	192.168.0.1	192.168.0.30	192.168.0.31
2	192.168.0.32/27	192.168.0.33	192.168.0.62	192.168.0.63
3	192.168.0.64/27	192.168.0.65	192.168.0.94	192.168.0.95
4	192.168.0.96/27	192.168.0.97	192.168.0.126	192.168.0.127
5	192.168.0.128/27	192.168.0.129	192.168.0.158	192.168.0.159
6	192.168.0.160/27	192.168.0.161	192.168.0.190	192.168.0.191
7	192.168.0.192/27	192.168.0.193	192.168.0.222	192.168.0.223
8	192.168.0.224/27	192.168.0.225	192.168.0.254	192.168.0.255

The IPv4 standard defines the portion of the IPv4 address range that is not routable on the internet and is suitable for private use, hence its name, the private IP address range. These three address ranges are defined solely for private use, that is, in the private addressing schemes using systems that are not directly connected to the internet. To be able to access the internet, a host configured with a private IP address needs to use **Network Address Translation** (**NAT**). This allows internal addresses to be mapped to one or more publicly available IP addresses. NAT helps keep an internal network isolated while addressing the shortage of publicly available IP addresses.

The following table shows the list of class A, B, and C private IP address ranges:

Network Class	Network	Range
A	10.0.0.0/8	10.0.0.0 – 10.255.255.255
B	172.16.0.0/12	172.16.0.0 –172.31.255.255
C	192.168.0.0/16	192.168.0.0 – 192.168.255.255

The private IP addresses are defined in RFC 1918, which is available at `http://tools.ietf.org/html/rfc1918`.

Configuring IPv6 addressing

Initially, the address space of 4,294,967,296 possible addresses (2^{32}) seemed inexhaustible and the address space was generously segmented and assigned. Back then, such thinking seemed reasonable because nobody expected the exponential growth of the internet or such a large number of connected devices. Nowadays, we are facing the depletion of the IPv4 address space, which was predicted years ago. The need for a solution to this problem led to development of the sixth generation of the IP protocol – IPv6. The IPv4 address is 32 bits long, while IPv6 uses 128-bit long addresses. Compared to IPv4, IPv6 has a four times larger address space of 2^{128}, or 340,282,366,920,938,463,463,374,607,431,768,211,456 addresses. This is significantly more than IPv4; however, IPv6 was not designed solely with host addressing in mind, but also to be able to accommodate newer 64-bit macOS addresses.

Converting from binary to hexadecimal notation

IPv4 addressing uses decimal notation and IPv6 uses hexadecimal notation, where the 128-bit address is divided into 16-bit chunks.

For example, the following number is a binary form of an IPv6 address:

```
00111101101011111001000000000010110000000000000100001110011100100100000000111
1111000000000000000000001010000111111101111111110101011
```

The 128-bit-long binary address number is divided into 16-bit-long chunks, as follows:

```
0011110110101111 0010000000001011 0000000000000100 0011110011110010
0100000011111110 0000000000000000 0101000011111110 1111111110101011
```

Each binary chunk is then converted to a hexadecimal format and the blocks are separated by colons:

```
3DAF:200B:0004:3CF2:40FE:0000:50FE:FFAB
```

The following table shows the decimal values and their corresponding hexadecimal and binary values:

Decimal	Hexadecimal	Binary
0	0	0000
1	1	0001
2	2	0010
3	3	0011
4	4	0100
5	5	0101
6	6	0110
7	7	0111
8	8	1000
9	9	1001
10	A	1010
11	B	1011
12	C	1100
13	D	1101
14	E	1110
15	F	1111

Zero suppression

IPv6 addresses are quite large; therefore, when multiple contiguous blocks of zeros occur, these can be shortened or substituted with a double colon, (::), which simplifies the address notation. For example, a contiguous block of zeros in the 3DAF:200B:0004:3CF2:40FE:0000:50FE:FFAB address can be shortened to a single zero, such as 3DAF:200B:0004:3CF2:40FE:0:50FE:FFAB, or by a double colon: 3DAF:200B:0004:3CF2:40FE::50FE:FFAB.

You can suppress the leading zeros of the 16-bit block as well, for example, 3DAF:200B:4:3CF2:40FE::50FE:FFAB.

Furthermore, only 16-bit contiguous blocks can be substituted or suppressed, and not parts of the 16-bit block; for instance, the FF04:30:0:0:0:0:0:4 address cannot be compressed to FF04:3::4. The unicast FF02:0:0:0:0:0:0:3 IPv6 address, on the other hand, can be shortened to FF02::3.

Similar to IPv4 address types, IPv6 also has different address types:

- **Unicast**: This address type represents a single interface or a node. It is used in one-to-one communications where one interface sends packets to a single receiver.

- **Multicast**: This address type represents multiple interfaces. It is used in a one-to-many communication model, where one sender sends packets to multiple recipients or interfaces on a network.
- **Anycast**: This address type represents multiple interfaces. It is used in a one-to-many-to-one communication model, where a sender sends a packet to multiple interfaces but a single interface is the recipient of the message. The one recipient that receives the message is defined as the nearest, being the one that is closest in terms of routing distance.

There are also other types of IPv6 addresses, as follows:

- **Global unicast**: Similar to IPv4 public addresses, these addresses are globally routable and reachable.
- **Link-local**: Hosts use link-local addresses to communicate with other hosts on the same network. The first 10 bits of a link-local address are always `1111 1110 10`, and the next 54 bits of a network address are always 0. The remaining 65 bits are interface ID bits that identify the host within a LAN. This creates the address prefix of `fe80::/64`.
- **Site-local**: These addresses are the same as the IPv4 private addresses. They can be used with private networks that do not have a direct IPv6 connection, and they can be used in addition to global addresses.
- **Unique local**: The unique local addresses are not routable on the internet, but they are routable between private network subnets.
- **Special IPv6 address**: These networks are reserved for special uses and purposes.
- **Transition addresses**: These addresses support the transition from IPv4 to IPv6:
    - **IPv4-compatible address**: This address type uses the `0:0:0:0:0:0:w.x.y.z` or `::w.x.y.z` format, where `w.x.y.z` is the dotted decimal IPv4 address notation. This type of address uses nodes that communicate with both IPv4 and IPv6 protocols.
    - **IPv4-mapped address:** This type of address uses IPv4-only nodes that can communicate with IPv6 nodes.
    - **6to4 address:** This type of address is used in communications between two nodes over the internet; the nodes use both IPv4 and IPv6.

For a better understanding of the relationship between IPv4 and IPv6, the following table compares the networking concepts and terminology of both standards:

IPv4 Address	IPv6 Address
Internet address classes	No such classes in IPv6
IPv4 multicast addresses (224.0.0.0/4)	IPv6 multicast addresses (FF00::/8)
Broadcast addresses: network broadcast, subnet broadcast, all-subnets directed broadcast, limited broadcast	No such addresses in IPv6
Unspecified address is 0.0.0.0	Unspecified address is ::
Loopback address is 127.0.0.1	Loopback address is ::1
Public IPv4 addresses	Global unicast addresses
Private IPv4 addresses (10.0.0.0/8, 172.16.0.0/12, and 192.168.0.0/16)	Site-local addresses (FEC0::/10)
APIPA addresses (169.254.0.0/16)	Link-local addresses (FE80::/64)
Address syntax: dotted decimal notation	Address syntax: colon hexadecimal format with suppression of leading zeros and zero compression. Embedded IPv4 addresses are expressed in dotted decimal notation.
Address prefix syntax: prefix length or dotted decimal (subnet mask) notation	Address prefix syntax: prefix length notation only

IPv6 autoconfiguration

One of the advantages of IPv6 over IPv4 is the capability to autoconfigure the client in the absence of the DHCP server. Although there is such a thing in IPv4 as autoconfiguration or **Automatic Private IP Addressing** (**APIPA**), it provides only local connectivity with no routing support. On the other hand, IPv6 autoconfiguration enables the IPv6 host to automatically configure itself without using an addressing protocol, such as DHCP for IPv6 or DHCPv6. By using IPv6 autoconfiguration, the IPv6 host can also autoconfigure other IPv6 addressing settings such as configuration parameters and the addresses of routers. Specifically, IPv6 autoconfiguration is specified in RFC 4862.

Autoconfiguration address states

There are three possible autoconfiguration address states, as follows:

- If an IPv6 node has an address autoconfiguration state that is **invalid**, then it can no longer receive or send unicast traffic. When an address lifetime expires, it enters the invalid state.
- If an IPv6 node has an address autoconfiguration state that is **valid**, then it means that it can send and receive unicast traffic. The Router Advertisement message determines the period that an address can exist in the valid state. The valid state itself can be preferred or deprecated. The address state is always equal to or greater than the preferred lifetime.
- If a node's address has been **verified** and it is unique, then the address enters the valid preferred state. A node can communicate on the network and can send and receive packets for the period of validity determined by the Router Advertisement message, that is, the time an address remains in the preferred and tentative states.
- If a node has a **valid** but **deprecated** address, it can still communicate and use the deprecated address, but this address is discouraged for new communications.

Autoconfiguration types

There are three autoconfiguration types, as follows:

- Autoconfiguration is completed through an address configuration protocol, such as **Dynamic Host Configuration Protocol v6** (**DHCPv6**). The autoconfiguration is stateful if a node gets configuration through Router Advertisement messages. This does not include the address prefixes that require the host to use and address the configuration protocol.
- Autconfiguration is stateful if a node has obtained an address through the Router Advertisement message and the address includes stateless address prefixes.
- Stateful and stateless autoconfiguration types; the host receives Router Advertisement messages that require hosts to use the address configuration protocol and includes stateless address prefixes.

The autoconfiguration process

An address autoconfiguration for an IPv6 host is performed and described in the following steps:

1. A host sends a Router Solicitation message.
2. If a host receives a Router Solicitation message, then it is configured using the information obtained in this message.
3. If a host does not receive a Router Solicitation message, then it can use the address configuration protocol (DHCPv6) to configure itself with the address and other configuration parameters.
4. The stateless address prefix and the 64-bit address identifier are both used to obtain a tentative address. The existence of a duplicate tentative address is verified during the process. If an address is not a duplicate, and, therefore, not in use, the address is initialized and a host obtains valid and preferred lifetimes in the Router Advertisement message.

Similar to DHCP for the configuration of IPv4 addresses, DHCPv6 also uses UDP messages, which DHCPv6 servers and relay agents listen for on UDP port 547. Unlike DHCP for IPv4, DHCPv6 has no broadcast addresses or messages.

The list of valid DHCPv6 messages and their comparison to DHCP IPV4 messages is shown in the following table:

DHCPv6 message	Description	DHCPv4 Equivalent
Solicit	This is sent by a client to locate servers.	DHCPDISCOVER
Advertise	This is sent by a server in response to a Solicit message to indicate availability.	DHCPOFFER
Request	This is sent by a client to request addresses or configuration settings from a specific server.	DHCPREQUEST
Confirm	This is sent by a client to all servers to determine whether a client's configuration is valid for the connected link.	DHCPREQUEST
Renew	This is sent by a client to a specific server to extend the lifetimes of assigned addresses and obtain updated configuration settings.	DHCPREQUEST
Rebind	This is sent by a client to any server when a response to the Renew message is not received.	DHCPREQUEST
Reply	This is sent by a server to a specific client in response to a Solicit, Request, Renew, Rebind, Information-Request, Confirm, Release, or Decline message.	DHCPACK
Release	This is sent by a client to indicate that the client is no longer using an assigned address.	DHCPRELEASE

Decline	This is sent by a client to a specific server to indicate that the assigned address is already in use.	DHCPDECLINE
Reconfigure	This is sent by a server to a client to indicate that the server has new or updated configuration settings. The client then sends either a Renew or Information-Request message.	N/A
Information-Request	This is sent by a client to request configuration settings (but not addresses).	DHCPINFORM
Relay-Forward	This is sent by a relay agent to forward a message to a server. The Relay-Forward message contains a client message encapsulated as the DHCPv6 Relay-Message option.	N/A
Relay-Reply	This is sent by a server to send a message to a client through a relay agent. Relay-Reply contains a server message that is encapsulated as the DHCPv6 Relay-Message option.	N/A

Implementing IPv6 stateless addressing

A typical DHCPv6 stateful host configuration includes the following exchange of messages in the process of obtaining an IPv6 address and configuration settings:

1. A client sends a Solicit message to locate the servers.
2. A server sends an Advertise message to indicate whether it is capable of providing IPv6 configuration settings and addresses.
3. A client sends a Request message to a server to request configuration settings and an address.
4. A server sends a Reply message that contains configuration settings and an address.

To configure a Windows Server 2016 DHCP role as a stateless DHCPv6 server, follow the following steps:

IPv4 and IPv6 interoperability

Interoperability between IPv4 and IPv6 addressing is often achieved and configured using transition technologies. The RFC 1752 contains the recommendations for the transition criteria such as new and existing host upgrades and configuration.

The definitions for the transition mechanisms for IPv6 hosts and routers are contained in the RFC 4213 document and the following addresses are defined to ease the transition process from IPv4 to IPv6:

- **IPv4-compatible addresses**: The IPv4-compatible address is used by nodes communicating with IPv6 over an IPv4-only infrastructure. The IPv6 traffic is encapsulated with an IPv4 header and sent to a destination host. The IPv4-compatible addresses support has been deprecated and it is not supported in Windows operating systems.
- **IPv4-mapped addresses**: The IPv4-mapped address, `0:0:0:0:0:FFFF:w.x.y.z` or `::FFFF:w.x.y.z`, is used for the internal representation of an IPv4 node to an IPv6 node. `w.x.y.z` is the dotted-decimal representation of a public IPv4 address.
- **Intra-Site Automatic Tunnel Addressing Protocol (ISATAP) addresses**: ISATAP addresses are defined in RFC 5214 and are composed of an `::0:5efe:w.x.y.z` interface identifier and a valid 64-bit unicast address prefix. If a node's address is based on a private IPv4 address, then `::0:5EFE:w.x.y.z` is used, where `w.x.y.z` is a private IPv4 address.

  Alternatively, if a node's address is a public IPv4 address, then `::200:5EFE:w.x.y.z` is used, where `w.x.y.z` is a public IPv4 address. ISATAP nodes do not require manual configuration to enable the functionality – it can be done automatically through Router Advertisement messages.

Enabling ISATAP is possible by using several methods, as follows:

- The `netsh` command. For example, use `netsh interface ipv6 isatap set router w.x.y.z`.
- By using the **GPO** or **Group Policy Objects** settings.
- By using **PowerShell**; you can use the following PowerShell command to configure ISATAP: `Set-NetIsatapConfiguration - Router w.x.y.z`.

- **6to4 addresses**: 6to4 addresses are defined in RFC 3056 and are based on the `002:WWXX:YYZZ::/48` prefix, where `WWXX:YYZZ` is the colon hexadecimal representation of `2001::/32`. 6to4 traffic is encapsulated with an IPv4 header and sent over an IPv4 network. Encapsulation or tunneling is done automatically on the sending and receiving end, or on a forwarding router.

A Windows Server 2016 computer can act as a 6to4 router by completing the following steps (using **Netsh** or **PowerShell**):

1. You can enable the 6to4 service as follows:
   - **Netsh**: `netsh interface 6to4 set state enabled`
   - **PowerShell**: `Set-Net6to4Coniguration -State Enabled`

2. You can enable forwarding on the 6to4 tunneling interface as follows:
   - **Netsh**: `netsh interface ipv6 set interface InterfaceNameOrIndex forwarding=enabled`
   - **PowerShell**: `Set-NetIPInterface -InterfaceAlias Name - AddressFamily IPv6 -Forwarding Enabled`

   Alternatively, enabling internet connection sharing automatically configures the server as a 6to4 router.

3. **Teredo addresses**: Teredo addresses are defined in RFC 4380 and are based on the prefix. They are used to create global IPv6 addresses for the nodes that are connected to the IPv4 network and provide support for NAT nodes. If, for example, your internal network is using private IPv4 addresses and you want to provide IPv6 connectivity though the internet, then Teredo is your choice as it supports NAT.

To configure Teredo, use the PowerShell `Set-NetTeredoConfiguration` cmdlet.

Configuring routing

To be able to forward the packets from one network to the other, Windows Server 2016 can act as a router for both IPv4 and IPv6 traffic, thanks to the built-in server role. In this way, the Windows Server 2016 computer can act on the network in a similar way to a hardware router device, with additional, Windows operating system-specific functionality. To be able to route traffic to and from different networks or subnets, you will need two or more physical network adapters.

Before you can configure a Windows Server 2016 as a router, you need to install a supporting role. To install a server role that supports routing, perform the following steps:

1. Open **Server Manager**.
2. Click on the **Manage** menu and choose **Add Roles and Features**.
3. On the **Before You Begin** screen, click on **Next**. To skip this page next time, select **Skip this page by default**.

4. On the **Installation Type** page, select **Role-based or feature-based installation**, and then click on **Next**.

5. On the **Server Selection** page, under **Server Pool**, make sure that the current server is selected. Alternatively, select the server on which you want to install the routing support role. Then, click on **Next**.

6. On the **Server Role** page, select the **Remote Access** role; then, click on **Next**:

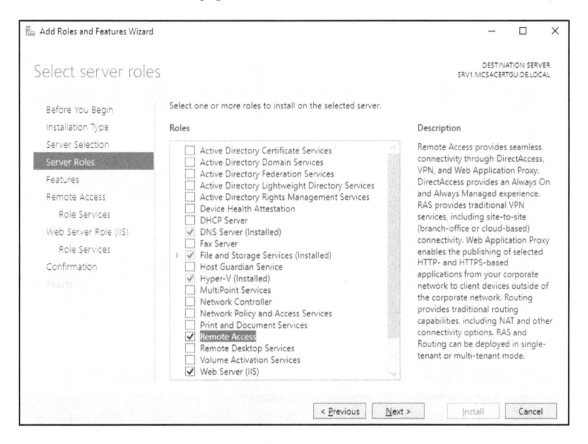

7. On the **Features** page, click on **Next**.

8. On the **Remote Access** page, read the information and then click on **Next**.

9. On the **Role Services** page, select **Routing**, and then click on **Add Features** if **Add Roles and Features Wizard** prompts you to install features required for the routing role:

10. The wizard automatically selects the **DirectAccess and VPN (RAS)** role and **Web Server Role (IIS)**; then, click on **Next**.
11. On the **Role services** page for **Web Server Role (IIS)**, click on **Next**.
12. On the **Confirmation** page, click on **Install**.
13. When the installation finishes, observe the installation progress page and click on **Close**.
14. After the installation finishes, observe the **Server Manager** window and the yellow triangle containing an exclamation mark near the flag.

15. Click on the flag and yellow triangle:

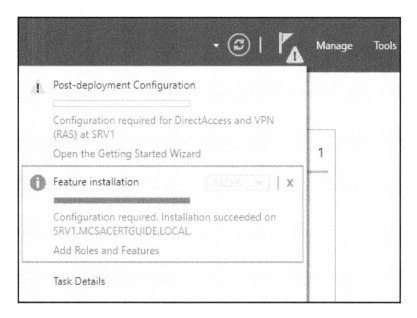

16. The menu shows that the installed **DirectAccess and VPN** role needs post-deployment configuration in order to be functional.

To configure Windows Server 2016 functionality as a router, perform the following steps:

1. Open **Server Manager**.
2. Click on the **Tools** menu and choose **Routing and Remote Access**.
3. The **Routing and Remote Access** window opens. Right-click on a server that you want to configure and choose **Configure and Enable Routing and Remote Access**.
4. The **Routing and Remote Access Server Setup Wizard** starts. Then, click on **Next**.

5. On the **Configuration** page, select **Custom configuration**, and then click on **Next**:

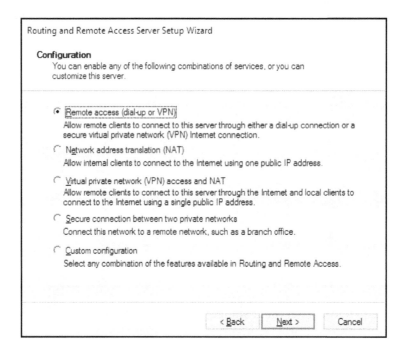

6. On the **Custom Configuration** page, select **LAN routing**, and then click on **Next**:

7. Click on **Finish**.
8. Now, wait a few seconds; when the **Routing and Remote Access** dialog box appears, click on **Start Service**.

To enable a routing protocol on a Windows Server 2016 operating system, complete the following steps:

1. Open **Server Manager**.
2. Click on the **Tools** menu and choose **Routing and Remote Access**.
3. Under the **IPv4** node, right-click on **General** and choose **New Routing Protocol...**:

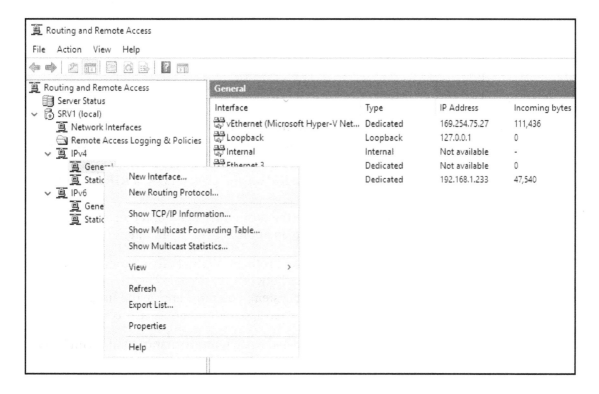

4. Select **RIP Version 2 for Internet Protocol** and click on **OK**:

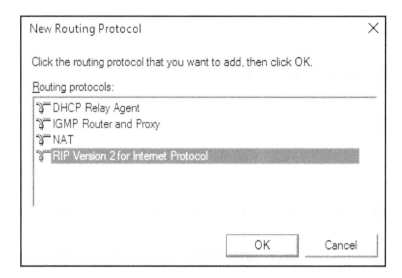

5. Note that you will not be able to add the RIP protocol if there are no usable network interfaces installed on a computer. Right-click on **RIP** and select **New Interface...**.
6. Choose a network interface to enable RIP on and click on **OK**; a **RIP Properties** page opens.
7. You can accept the defaults, or make the desired changes, and then click on **OK** to enable the RIP routing protocol on an applicable network interface.

Windows Server 2016 supports **Border Gateway Protocol** (**BGP**). BGP is a dynamic routing protocol, which means that it "learns" the routes between connected sites. To install BGP support in the Windows Server 2016 operating system, you must enable the support for each tenant using the PowerShell `Enable-RemoteAccessRoutingDomain` command.

The following example demonstrates how to install RAS in multitenancy mode with VPN, RAS, and BGP support:

```
$Sample_RoutingDomain = "SampleTenant"
Install-RemoteAccess -MultiTenancy
Enable-RemoteAccessRoutingDomain -Name $Sample_RoutingDomain -Type All -
PassThru
```

To enable BGP only, without multitenancy capabilities, use the following PowerShell command:

```
Install-RemoteAccess -VpnType RoutingOnly
```

Summary

In this chapter, we looked at IPv4 addressing and options. We learned about the different internet address classes. Then, we looked at interoperability and routing in the Windows Server 2016 operating system. In the next chapter, we will proceed with the installation of the DNS server role.

Configuring DNS 2

In the second chapter, we will cover the **Domain Name System** (**DNS**) support and server role in the Windows Server 2016 operating system. After implementing IP addressing correctly, we can proceed with the installation of the DNS server role. This chapter explains the DNS installation requirements and proceeds on to more advanced topics that are needed for the DNS to function correctly. These include the configuration of root hints, forwarders, and DNS policies, and the configuration and management of zones and records.

In this chapter, we will cover the following topics:

- Installing DNS servers
- Configuring DNS servers
- Configuring DNS zones

Technical requirements

As mentioned in the previous chapter, in order to build your own lab, you will need the Windows Server 2016 operating system – either the Standard edition or the Enterprise edition. In order to build a lab to prepare for the exam, you can use Hyper-V on Windows Server or the Windows client operating systems. You can practice on real hardware as well, but it is more convenient and time-effective to practice in a virtualized environment. Any virtualization environment or hypervisor will do, and you can set up a practice lab in Microsoft Azure as well.

Installing DNS servers

In this section, we will address the requirements for installing the DNS server role in Windows Server 2016. Before we proceed, let's take a look at name resolution fundamentals.

Windows Server and the Windows client operating systems use name resolution to translate or map numerical IP addresses – which are used for **Transmission Control Protocol/Internet Protocol (TCP/IP)** communication – to computer names, which are easier to remember. Windows operating systems use two types of names in name resolution: **host names** and **NetBIOS names**.

For resolving host names to IP addresses, Windows operating systems DNS is used, and for resolving NetBIOS names, **Windows Internet Name Service (WINS)** is used. The hostname can contain letters, numbers, hyphens, and periods, and can be up to 255 characters long. Hostname can exist in nickname form or domain name form. Domain names are structured names in a hierarchical namespace, while nicknames are the aliases of an IP address. Unlike host names, NetBIOS names are not hierarchical and are 16-byte long addresses that are used to identify NetBIOS resources on the network.

The name resolution of choice in Windows operating systems is *DNS* rather than *WINS* because of its advantages and tight integration with Active Directory.

Domain name resolution overview

DNS is the part of the TCP/IP protocol suite and, more specifically, it is a part of the application layer.

The following diagram shows the TCP/IP layer model, the TCP/IP protocol suite, and the DNS protocol position, among other protocols:

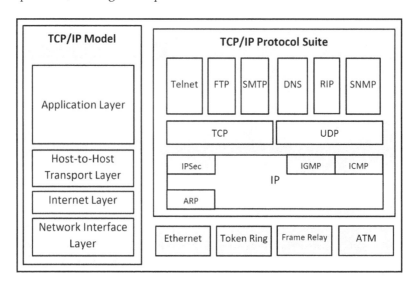

The DNS namespace is based on a hierarchical and logical model and uses a series of messages that are sent over either **User Datagram Protocol** (**UDP**) port 53 or TCP port 53. UDP is the primary protocol for DNS operations because it is faster.

The DNS consists of three main components:

- The domain namespace and resource records
- The nameservers
- The resolvers

The domain namespace and resource records

The DNS architecture is designed as a hierarchical, distributed database that uses mechanisms for querying and updating the database, including replicating the database among other servers hosting the DNS server role.

The DNS database consists of records or information about the hosts and resources in a domain, and information about a domain structure. For example, clients rely on the information from the DNS server database in order to obtain an IP address that is associated to a DNS name.

The following table shows the details of the most common resource records:

Resource type	Description	Resource data	Time To Live (TTL) value
SOA	Start of Authority	The owner name The primary nameserver DNS name and serial number The refresh interval The retry interval The expiry time The minimum TTL	The default TTL is 60 minutes.
A	IPv4 host	The owner name (the host DNS name) The host IPv4 address	Record-specific TTL if present, otherwise, zone (SOA) TTL.
AAAA	IPv6 host	The owner name (the host DNS name) The host IPv6 address	Record-specific TTL if present, otherwise, zone (SOA) TTL.
NS	Nameserver	The owner name The nameserver DNS name	Record-specific TTL if present, otherwise, zone (SOA) TTL.

MX	**Mail Exchanger**	The owner name The MX server DNS name, preference number	Record-specific TTL if present, otherwise, zone (SOA) TTL.
CNAME	**Canonical Name** (an alias)	The owner name (the alias name) The host DNS name	Record-specific TTL if present, otherwise, zone (SOA) TTL.

Nameservers

Nameservers are computers that store DNS databases in order to assist in a DNS resolution process; that is, in a process to obtain an IP address for a resource or a host. Alternatively, they store information about DNS zones, which is a way to organize an authoritative namespace.

Resolvers

Resolvers are applications that run on DNS servers and DNS clients, and initiate queries to obtain information from DNS servers. A DNS server uses a resolver to resolve a query on behalf of a DNS client, while a DNS client uses a resolver to create a DNS name query.

DNS names

DNS names have the following characteristics:

- A **Fully Qualified Domain Name** (**FQDN**) consists of a series of names – the leftmost name is a host or a resource name, and the rightmost domain name is a root domain.
- According to RFC 1034, FQDNs can only consist of the characters a-z, A-Z, 0-9, and the minus or dash (-) sign. RFC 2181 allows the use of other characters as well, but it is strongly advised to use the names that are described in RFC 1034.
- FQDNs are not case-sensitive.
- The maximum length of an FQDN cannot exceed 255 characters.
- Each name within an FQDN cannot exceed 63 characters.
- In an FQDN, each name is separated by a period (.).
- An FQDN ends with a period (.), which represents the root domain.

The DNS domain name consists of individual domain name labels separated by dots, from an individual hostname to the root of a domain. In this way, a host can be uniquely identified within a domain namespace and a name like this is defined as FQDN. An example of an FQDN for the host computer named
SRV1 is `SRV1.research.stockholm.itdemolabs.com`.

DNS hierarchy

The following diagram shows the DNS hierarchy. The `SRV1` host computer FQDN clearly states its position within a domain space. The first level domains (that is, **eu**, **org**, **edu**, and **com**) are managed by the registration authority and each further domain level namespace is managed by the respective domain name authority. In this example, the second level domains (that is, **Microsoft**, **GitHub**, **Google**, and **ITDemoLabs**) are managed by the `.com` domain authority, while the other respective domains manage their own names under their namespace. The **ITDemoLabs** domain has authority over only the domain namespace that it controls, meaning that it manages domain names under its control, such as **Marketing** or **Research**. The **Research** domain contains the **SRV1** host, which is referenced by its own FQDN:

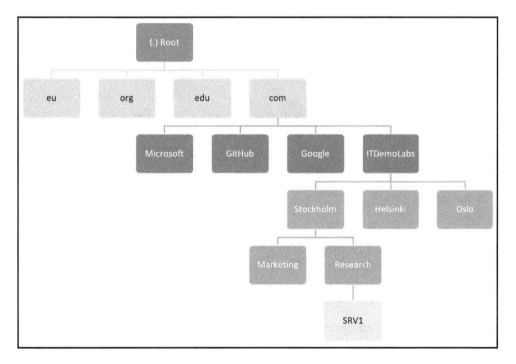

There are five types of domain names used in the DNS:

1. **The root domain**: The root domain represents the top of the tree and it is the highest level in a domain namespace. It is represented by a period (.); an FQDN also contains a root domain, as this allows it to define an exact location in a domain namespace or in a domain tree. For example, `oslo.itdemolabs.com` is an FQDN, while `oslo.itemolabs.com` is not.

2. **The top level domain**: This domain name belongs to countries (such as co.uk, de, and se), regions (such as eu), types of organizations (such as gov, mil, and org), and, more recently, to domain types (such as info, online, tech, and space).

3. **The second level domain**: This domain name is registered to an organization or to an individual (such as `microsoft.com` or `kranjac.eu`).

4. **The subdomain**: These domain name(s) can be created by a second level domain owner in order to divide a domain namespace into logical, departmental, and geographical locations. A subdomain can be further divided into child subdomains or next-in-level subdomains, allowing a namespace to grow not only horizontally but vertically as well. An example of a subdomain is `research29.kranjac.eu`.

5. **The hostname** or **resource name**: A host or a resource name identifies a specific resource or endpoint in a domain or on a network. An example of a hostname or a resource name is `SRV1` and its FQDN is `srv1.research29.kranjac.eu`.

DNS queries

Hostnames or resource names are also called **resource records** (**RRs**), and are kept in a database. They are maintained and accessed by a nameserver or a server that is hosting a DNS server role in a Microsoft Windows Server ecosystem. A client can query a nameserver with two types of DNS queries, as follows:

- Recursive
- Iterative

A DNS server responds to a recursive query with either a successful response or a failure response. With a recursive query, a DNS server must query other DNS servers in order to resolve a request if it does not know the answer, that is, if it is not an authority for the domain or if the results of the query are not in its cache.

A DNS server responds to an iterative query with the best response that it has, either based on the cache or based on the local zone (database) information. For example, it might respond with an IP address of an authoritative DNS server for the next-in-level subdomain.

How DNS works

The following diagram demonstrates the process of a client accessing a web page (www.microsoft.com) and the process of querying a DNS in order to obtain an IP address of a web server, or the www host:

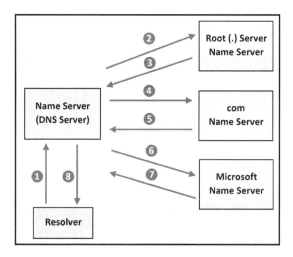

Considering the preceeding diagram, the process of querying a DNS can be explained as follows:

1. The client performs a recursive query to the default **Name Server** for www.microsoft.com.
2. The default **Name Server** performs an iterative query for www.microsoft.com.
3. The **Root (.) Server** returns a response (or a referral) containing a **com Name Server** IP address.
4. The **Name Server** performs an iterative query for www.microsoft.com.
5. The **com Name Server** returns a response containing the **Microsoft Name Server** IP address.
6. The **Name Server** performs an iterative query for www.microsoft.com.
7. The microsoft.com nameserver returns a response containing a www nameserver IP address.
8. The default **Name Server** returns a response to an original **Resolver** (client) query with an IP address of a www host, which is a www.microsoft.com web server.

Installing the DNS server role

Before proceeding to install the DNS role, it is recommended that you configure the target server with a static IP address. If a DNS server is configured with a dynamic IP address, then that means a DNS server might get a new IP address and the clients that have an incorrect DNS server address won't be able to resolve the DNS name.

Installing the DNS server role using Server Manager

To install the DNS server role on a computer running the Windows Server 2016 operating system using Server Manager, complete the following steps:

1. Open Server Manager.
2. From the **Manage** menu, select **Add Roles and Features**.
3. On the **Before You Begin** page, click on **Next**.
4. Select **Role-based or feature-based installation**. Then, click on **Next**.
5. On the **Select destination server** page, select the current server or a remote server from the server pool, and then click on **Next**.
6. On the **Select Server roles** page, select the **DNS Server** role. When the **Add Roles and Feature Wizard** page appears, click on **Add Features** to add the features required for the DNS server role. Then, click on **Next**:

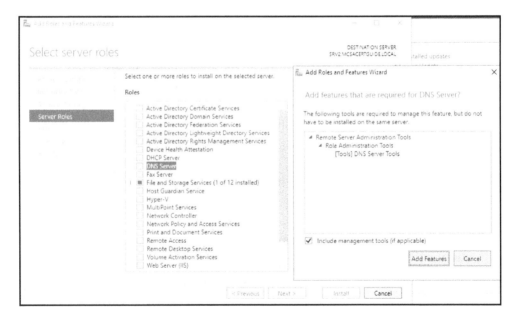

7. On the **Select Features** page, click on **Next**. You already accepted the required features in the previous step, so click on **Next**.
8. On the **DNS Server** page, read the information and then click on **Next**.
9. On the **Confirm installation selections** page, click on **Install**.
10. When the installation finishes, review the results and click on **Close**. The **DNS Server** role feature is installed.

Installing the DNS server role using PowerShell

Even if using Server Manager seems relatively quick and straightforward, you can install the DNS server role and the required management tools using PowerShell even more quickly and easily. To install the DNS server role using PowerShell, use the `Add-WindowsFeature DNS -IncludeManagementTools` command. The following screenshot shows a PowerShell window containing information after a successful DNS server role installation, including the relevant management tools:

```
Administrator: Windows PowerShell

Windows PowerShell
Copyright (C) 2016 Microsoft Corporation. All rights reserved.

PS C:\Users\administrator.MCSACERTGUIDE> Add-WindowsFeature DNS -IncludeManagementTools

Success Restart Needed Exit Code    Feature Result
------- -------------- ---------    --------------
True    No             Success      {DNS Server, Remote Server Administration ...

PS C:\Users\administrator.MCSACERTGUIDE> _
```

In the next section, we will learn how to configure DNS servers.

Configuring DNS servers

After installing the DNS server role on a Windows Server computer, you need to configure the DNS server role before a server can respond to name resolution queries, store database copies, and perform other relevant DNS server tasks.

Configuring the DNS server

To perform an initial DNS server configuration, complete the following steps:

1. Open **Server Manager**, click on the **Tools** menu, and then click on **DNS.** Alternatively, open the **Start** menu, expand **Windows Administrative Tools**, and then click on **DNS**.

2. A **DNS Manager** window opens; under the **DNS** node, a current server name is displayed. In this example, **SRV2** is a local server on which a DNS server role is installed.

3. Right-click on the server name and click on **Configure a DNS Server...**, as shown in the following screenshot:

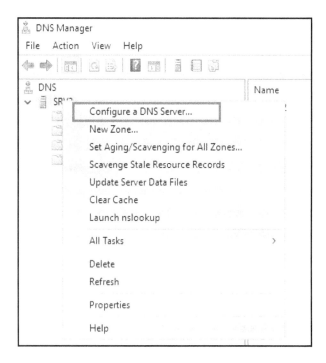

4. **Configure a DNS Server Wizard** starts; click on **Next**.

5. In **Select Configuration Action**, there are three possible choices:
   - **Create a forward lookup zone**
   - **Create a forward and reverse lookup zones**
   - **Configure root hints only**

We will explain root hints, forward, and reverse lookup zones later in this chapter. In this simple example, we will choose the first option and create a forward lookup zone, as this will enable our DNS server to host a zone, resource records, and respond to hostname resolution queries. Then, click on **Next**:

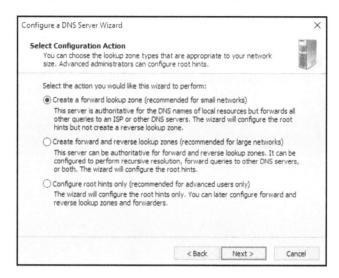

6. On the **Primary Server Location** page, you need to choose which server has authority for the forward lookup zone that you are configuring, or which server holds and maintains a name database for the zone. You have the option to make this server authoritative for a new zone or configure the server to hold a copy of a zone and create a secondary forward lookup zone. Choose **This server maintains the zone** and then click on **Next**:

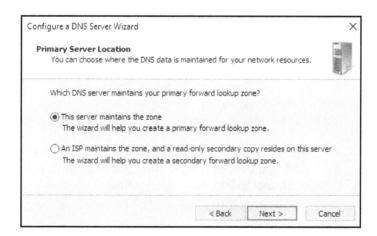

7. On the **Zone Name** page, you must specify what part of a DNS namespace this server will have authority over. We will choose the `labpc.mcsacertguide.local` zone and configure the SRV2 server to be an authority for the given zone. Type the zone name in the **Zone Name** field and then click on **Next**:

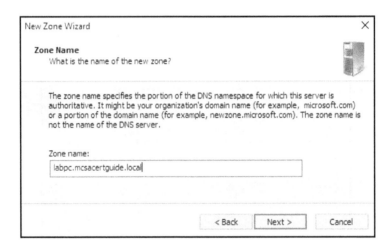

8. On the **Zone File** page, the **Create a new file with this file name** field is already populated with the appropriate filename for the zone. Notice that the second option gives you the option to import the existing zone file. Review the page and then click on **Next**.

9. The **Dynamic Update** page lets you select the type of dynamic updates that you want to allow into the zone:

   - The first option allows the zone updates only from Active Directory Domain Controllers, if a zone is an Active Directory-integrated zone. In this example, this option is unavailable because the server is not an Active Directory Domain Controller and the zone is not an Active Directory-integrated zone. This option allows clients to update their resource records in a secure, dynamic, and automatic way.

   - The second option allows any client to update its resource records in the zone and it is the most unsecure option.

   - The third option does not allow any kind of dynamic updates and you must add, remove, or update resource records in the zone manually. Choose **Do not allow dynamic updates** and then click on **Next**, as shown in the following screenshot:

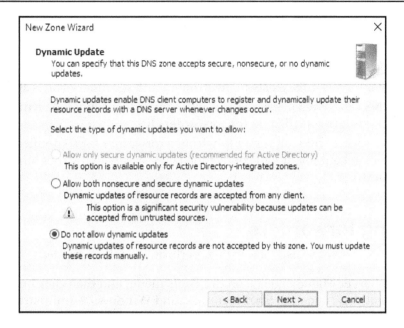

10. On the **Forwarders** page, choose **No**, so that it should not forward queries and then click on **Next**. We will explain forwarders later in this chapter. The **Searching for Root Hints** window appears and, after a few seconds, **Completing the Configure a DNS Server Wizard** is displayed, showing a summary of the configuration.

11. Review the configuration and then click on **Finish**. You have successfully completed the configuration of a DNS Server.

Configuring root hints, recursion, and forwarders

In a DNS, a forwarder is a server that is delegated to forward DNS queries for external names to DNS servers outside of a network. A server can act as a forwarder to resolve all external DNS queries or to resolve DNS queries for specific domains. A server is not configured as a forwarder, rather it is selected by configuring other DNS servers to forward specific DNS queries that they are unable to resolve.

In a configuration without a forwarder, DNS servers send name resolution queries using root hints. This can potentially be a security issue as some internal information might be revealed, leading to unnecessary traffic. When using a forwarder, or multiple computers designated as forwarders, these are responsible for resolving external names and act as an intermediary between on-premises and the outside world, limiting the exposure of internal resources to the internet.

When a Windows Server 2016 DNS is configured to use forwarding, it resolvies DNS names in the following way:

1. A DNS server receives a name resolution query from a DNS client and checks whether the resource exists in the primary and secondary zones and in its cache.
2. If a DNS cannot resolve a query, it will forward, or send, the recursive query to the forwarders specified on the forwarders list.
3. A DNS server will wait for a reply from a forwarder for a specified time. If it does not get a reply, it will contact the DNS servers in the root hints list for name resolution.

Configuring forwarders

To configure a DNS server to use forwarding, perform the following steps:

1. Open **Server Manager**, click on the **Tools** menu, and then click on **DNS**. Alternatively, open the **Start** menu, expand **Windows Administrative Tools** and click on **DNS**.
2. A **DNS Manager** window opens. Right-click on the server name and then click on **Properties**.
3. Click on the **Forwarders** tab:

4. The configuration shows the list of DNS servers IP addresses that will act as forwarders. If forwarders are not available and you want to disable the use of root hints servers for name resolution, then clear the checkbox next to the **Edit...** button.

5. To configure and manage the forwarders, click on the **Edit...** button:

6. Type in the IP address or FQDN of a DNS server that you want to use as a forwarder and arrange them in the list by order of preference using the <u>U</u>p and D<u>o</u>wn buttons.

7. To adjust the number of seconds before forward queries time out, enter the number in the lower field. Enter a larger number if you notice that the forwarders take longer than usual to respond to queries. Alternatively, if your configuration supports more forwarders, then add more forwarders to the list.

8. Click on the **OK** button twice to close all the windows and accept the changes.

Configuring conditional forwarders

To configure conditional forwarders for specific domain queries, perform the following steps:

1. Open **DNS Manager**.

2. In the left pane, right-click on **Conditional Forwarders** and then click on **New Conditional Forwarder...**, as shown in the following screenshot:

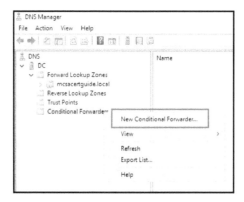

3. A **New Conditional Forwarder** window opens.

4. In a **DNS Domain** field, enter the name of the domain to which the queries will be forwarded to the servers on the list:

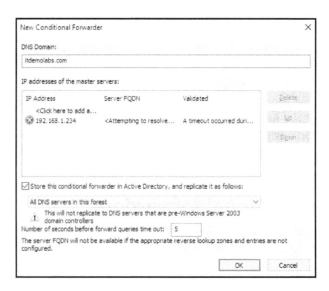

5. To configure the replication of the conditional forwarders list for a given domain, select the **Store this conditional forwarder in Active Directory, and replicate it as follows** checkbox. You can configure the replication to all the DNS servers in this forest, to all the DNS servers in this domain, or to all the domain controllers in this domain.

6. Additionally, configure the number of seconds before the forward queries time out by modifying the default value.

7. Click on the **OK** button twice to close all windows and accept the changes.

Configuring root hints

Root hints is a list of root DNS servers used to discover authoritative servers. Although Windows Server 2016 already has a list of root hints servers, a DNS wizard tries to update the root hints list during the DNS configuration process. If the update was unsuccessful, then the list can be edited and updated later.

To configure root hints, complete the following procedure:

1. Open DNS Manager.
2. In the left pane, right-click on a server name and click on **Properties**.
3. Click on the **Root Hints** tab:

4. You can edit the list of root nameservers, and add or remove servers from the list. Alternatively, to copy the list of nameservers from another DNS server, click on the **Copy from Server** button.

5. Specify the IP address or DNS name of the server containing an updated list of root nameservers that you want to copy to the current DNS server and click on **OK**.

6. Click on the **OK** button to accept the changes.

Configuring recursion

We already know that DNS servers can perform two types of name resolution or DNS queries: iterative or recursive. In a recursive query, DNS servers ask other servers on behalf of other servers, while using an iterative query, and DNS servers reply with a "best answer," that is, with a referral to a "next-in-line" authoritative NS. Although recursive queries are enabled by default, this is not always the best security practice, as it leaves the DNS server vulnerable to a denial-of-service attack. To prevent this, it is recommended that you disable recursive queries on a DNS server; however, this will also disable the forwarders.

To disable recursion on a DNS server, complete the following steps:

1. Open DNS Manager.
2. In the left pane, right-click on a server name and click on **Properties**.
3. Click on the **Advanced** tab.
4. Select the **Disable recursion (also disabled forwarders)** checkbox:

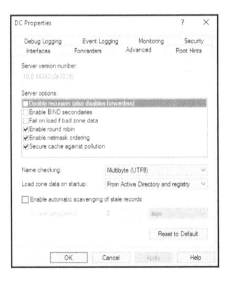

5. Click on **OK** to accept the changes and close the properties window.

Configuring advanced DNS settings

The DNS server role is an important, fundamental infrastructure role and, as such, needs adequate attention. As with any other technology in Windows Server 2016, a thousand pages would not be enough to describe every feature in detail, but there are a few other configuration settings that are worth mentioning.

To configure advanced DNS features, open DNS Manager, and in the left-hand pane, right-click on a server name, and then click on **Properties**. This opens the DNS properties page for the current DNS server and has several tabs containing more advanced DNS options. The following are the tabs that we will be looking into:

- Interfaces
- Debug Logging
- Event Logging
- Monitoring
- Security

Interfaces

By default, the DNS server listens for DNS requests on all available network interfaces, on both IPv4 and IPv6 networks. To limit DNS server responses only to select IP addresses, select the appropriate radio button, as shown in the screenshot given here:

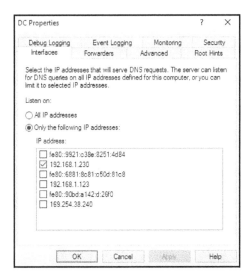

Once the appropriate button is selected, we can then check the network addresses that the DNS server will respond to the name resolution queries on.

Debug Logging

Debug Logging is disabled by default; to enable debug logging, select the **Log packets for debugging** checkbox. This will enable you to collect the details of the packets sent to and from the DNS server in the specified log file, which can be accessed later for troubleshooting purposes:

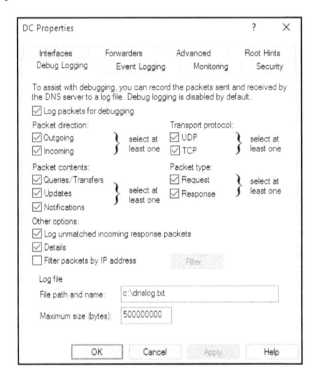

The preceding screenshot shows the **Debug Logging** tab, the logging of packets enabled, and the configured dnslog.txt log file in the root directory of the C: drive. A sample of data collected in a log file is shown in the following screenshot:

```
dnslog - Notepad                                                    —    □    ×
File  Edit  Format  View  Help
     CD       0                                                              ^
     AD       0
     RCODE    0 (NOERROR)
 QCOUNT    1
 ACOUNT    0
 NSCOUNT   1
 ARCOUNT   1
 QUESTION SECTION:
 Offset = 0x000c, RR count = 0
 Name      "(4)SRV1(13)MCSACERTGUIDE(5)LOCAL(0)"
     QTYPE    SOA (6)
     QCLASS   1
 ANSWER SECTION:
     empty
 AUTHORITY SECTION:
 Offset = 0x002a, RR count = 0
 Name      "[C011](13)MCSACERTGUIDE(5)LOCAL(0)"
     TYPE    SOA  (6)
     CLASS   1
     TTL     3600
     DLEN    38
     DATA
             PrimaryServer: (2)dc[C011](13)MCSACERTGUIDE(5)LOCAL(0)
             Administrator: (10)hostmaster[C011](13)MCSACERTGUIDE(5)LOCAL(0)    SerialNo    = 242
             Refresh     = 900
             Retry       = 600
             Expire      = 86400
             MinimumTTL  = 3600
 ADDITIONAL SECTION:
 Offset = 0x005c, RR count = 0
 Name      "[C036](2)dc[C011](13)MCSACERTGUIDE(5)LOCAL(0)"
     TYPE    A  (1)
     CLASS   1
     TTL     3600
     DLEN    4
     DATA    192.168.1.230                                                     v
```

Event Logging

The **Event Logging** tab contains the settings that are required to configure the level of event logging for the DNS server operation. It is recommended to log all the events in order to perform comprehensive server performance analysis if required:

Monitoring

The **Monitoring** tab has the option to verify the configuration of the DNS server by performing manual or automatic tests. The tests consist of a simple DNS query against the DNS server, and a recursive query to the other DNS servers. To perform the test once, select the appropriate checkboxes, and then click on **Test Now**:

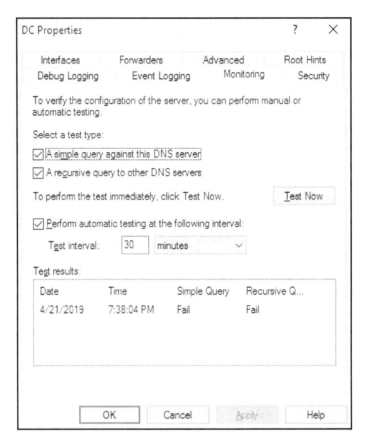

To perform automatic testing at the predefined intervals, select the automatic testing checkbox, select the interval, and then click on **Apply**. The **Test** results pane will show the type of tests performed and the results of these tests.

Security

One of the most important parts of administering a DNS server role is defining suitable access rights for the right people. This page is well-known as it is almost identical when configuring access control lists for any other resource on Windows Server or Windows client operating system. Here, you can granularly configure access rights to groups or users for all DNS server operations:

Administering the DNS with PowerShell

Administering the DNS server with PowerShell is significantly faster and easier.

In Windows Server 2016, several new PowerShell parameters and cmdlets were introduced, as follows:

- `Add-DnsServerRecursionScope`: This cmdlet creates a new recursion scope on the DNS server. Recursion scopes are used by DNS policies to specify a list of forwarders to be used in a DNS query.
- `Remove-DnsServerRecursionScope`: This cmdlet removes existing recursion scopes.
- `Set-DnsServerRecursionScope`: This cmdlet changes the settings of an existing recursion scope.
- `Get-DnsServerRecursionScope`: This cmdlet retrieves information about an existing recursion scope.
- `Add-DnsServerClientSubnet`: This cmdlet creates a new DNS client subnet. Subnets are used by DNS policies to identify where a DNS client is located.
- `Remove-DnsServerClientSubnet`: This cmdlet removes existing DNS client subnets.
- `Set-DnsServerClientSubnet`: This cmdlet changes the settings of an existing DNS client subnet.
- `Get-DnsServerClientSubnet`: This cmdlet retrieves information about existing DNS client subnets.
- `Add-DnsServerQueryResolutionPolicy`: This cmdlet creates a new DNS query resolution policy. DNS query resolution policies are used to specify if and how a query is responded to, based on different criteria.
- `Remove-DnsServerQueryResolutionPolicy`: This cmdlet removes existing DNS policies.
- `Set-DnsServerQueryResolutionPolicy`: This cmdlet changes the settings of an existing DNS policy.
- `Get-DnsServerQueryResolutionPolicy`: This cmdlet retrieves information about existing DNS policies.
- `Enable-DnsServerPolicy`: This cmdlet enables existing DNS policies.
- `Disable-DnsServerPolicy`: This cmdlet disables existing DNS policies.

- `Add-DnsServerZoneTransferPolicy`: This cmdlet creates a new DNS server zone transfer policy. DNS zone transfer policies specify whether to deny or ignore a zone transfer based on different criteria.
- `Remove-DnsServerZoneTransferPolicy`: This cmdlet removes existing DNS server zone transfer policies.
- `Set-DnsServerZoneTransferPolicy`: This cmdlet changes the settings of an existing DNS server zone transfer policy.
- `Get-DnsServerResponseRateLimiting`: This cmdlet retrieves RRL settings.
- `Set-DnsServerResponseRateLimiting`: This cmdlet changes RRL settings.
- `Add-DnsServerResponseRateLimitingExceptionlist`: This cmdlet creates an RRL exception list on the DNS server.
- `Get-DnsServerResponseRateLimitingExceptionlist`: This cmdlet retrieves RRL exception lists.
- `Remove-DnsServerResponseRateLimitingExceptionlist`: This cmdlet removes an existing RRL exception list.
- `Set-DnsServerResponseRateLimitingExceptionlist`: This cmdlet changes RRL exception lists.
- `Add-DnsServerResourceRecord`: This cmdlet was updated to support unknown record types.
- `Get-DnsServerResourceRecord`: This cmdlet was updated to support unknown record types.
- `Remove-DnsServerResourceRecord`: This cmdlet was updated to support unknown record types.
- `Set-DnsServerResourceRecord`: This cmdlet was updated to support unknown record types.

 You can find out more information at `https://docs.microsoft.com/en-us/windows-server/networking/dns/what-s-new-in-dns-server`.

Configuring DNS zones

DNS organizes and manages the namespace database in a specific physical structure using zones. Zones are physical namespace boundaries that contain information about one or more domains and their members:

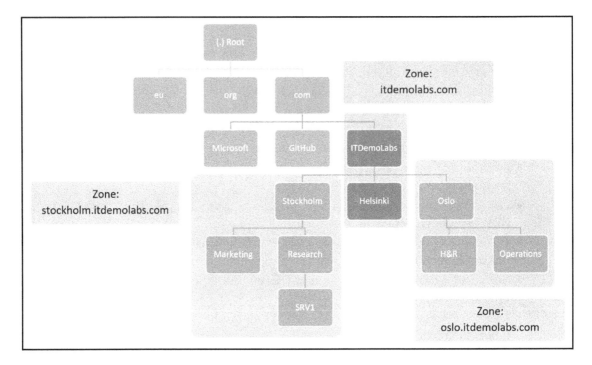

For example, the `itdemolabs.com` zone contains both the `itdemolabs.com` and `helsinki.itdemolabs.com` domains. Other domains are stored and managed in two separate zones, with each having its own separate zone database.

There are three types of DNS zones, as follows:

- **Primary zone**: This is the original zone, or the first created copy of a database, where all zone resources are managed.
- **Secondary zone**: This is the read-only copy of the primary zone and it is updated and managed using zone updates and zone transfers from the primary zone.
- **Stub zone**: This is the read-only copy of the primary zone database that contains only the resource records needed to locate the authoritative DNS server for the domain.

In addition to forward lookup zones, which resolve DNS names to IP addresses, reverse lookup zones resolve IP addresses to DNS names. Both forward and reverse lookup zones can be set up as a primary, a secondary, or a stub zone.

Configuring DNS primary zones

To create a primary forward lookup zone, complete the following steps:

1. Open DNS Manager.
2. In the left-hand pane, right-click on the **Forward Lookup Zone** and then click on **New Zone**.
3. **New Zone Wizard** starts; now click on **Next**.
4. On the **Zone Type** page, select the type of the zone that you want to create. In addition to the primary, secondary, and stub zones, there is an option to store the zone in Active Directory. This option is only available if a DNS server is a domain controller and can enhance the security and replication performance. Select the **Primary zone** radio button and click on **Next**:

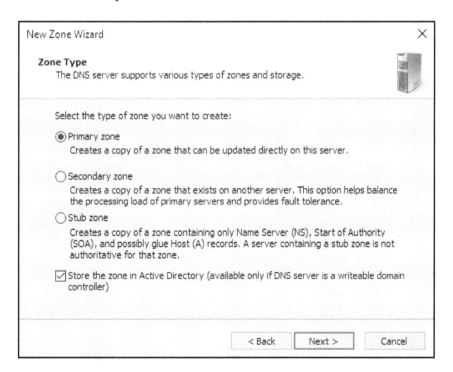

5. The **Active Directory Zone Replication Scope** page is only available if you checked the option to store the zone in Active Directory in the previous step. By default, the zone information will be replicated to all DNS servers running on domain controllers in the current domain. The other two radio buttons allow you to choose replication to all the DNS servers running on domain controllers in the forest and to replicate data to all the domain controllers in this domain (for backward compatibility); leave the defaults as they are and click on **Next**:

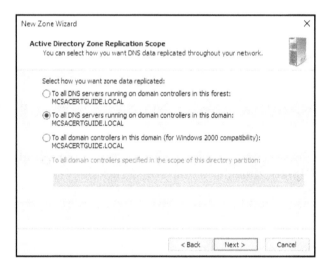

6. On the **Zone Name** page, type in the zone name that you are creating. In this example, we will choose `lab1.mcsacertguide.local` as a zone name; then, click on **Next**:

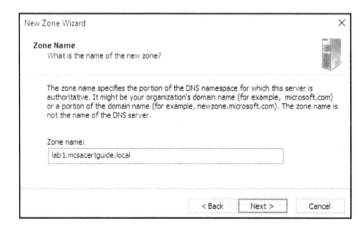

7. On the **Dynamic Update** page, select the allowed types of dynamic updates to the zone. Along with the option not to allow zone updates, two choices are available. First, to allow only secure updates to the zone, which is recommended for integration with Active Directory, and second, to allow both secure and nonsecure dynamic updates. The latter option will accept zone changes even from unknown sources, which is not secure and, therefore, an undesired option. Leave the default option selected (to allow secure updates) if you have Active Directory available. If not, choose the appropriate option from the other two choices, and then click on **Next**:

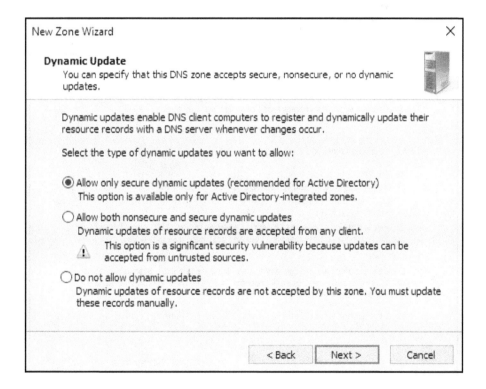

8. Review the summary in the last step and click on **Finish** to create the primary zone and close the wizard.

Open DNS Manager and click on a newly created zone. Consider the records that are created in the zone: the SOA record and the nameserver record.

Configuring DNS secondary zones

To configure a secondary forward lookup zone for redundancy and additional availability, complete the following steps on the server (other than the server hosting the primary zone) that you want to replicate:

1. Open DNS Manager.
2. In the left-hand pane, right-click on the **Forward Lookup Zones** and click on **New Zone**.
3. **New Zone Wizard** starts; now click on **Next**.
4. On the **Zone Type** page, select the **Secondary zone** and then click on **Next**:

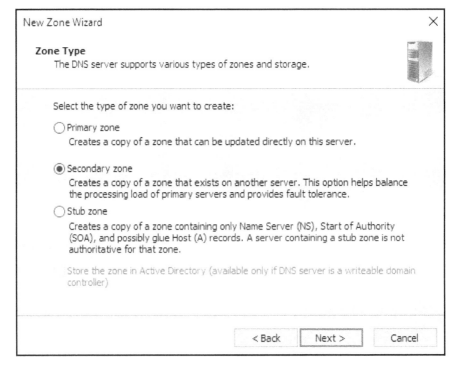

5. Type the name of the primary zone that you want to replicate. We will choose the `lab1.mcsacertguide.local` zone that was created in the previous example. Then, click on **Next**.

6. On **Master DNS Servers**, type in the FQDN or IP address of the server from which you want to replicate the primary zone. If you type the FQDN of the server, **New Zone Wizard** automatically resolves the name to an IPv4 address and then tries to resolve the name to an IPv6 address as well. If you did not set up IPv6 addressing, a red **X** icon prevents you from clicking on **Next** as the button is grayed out:

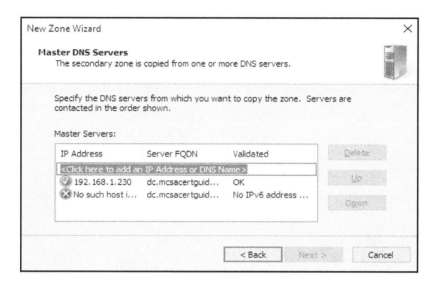

7. Select the IPv6 validation text line with a red **X** icon and click on **Delete**. Then, click on **Next**.
8. Review the changes and click on **Finish** to close the wizard.
9. In **DNS Manager**, observe the error stating **Zone Not Loaded by DNS Server**:

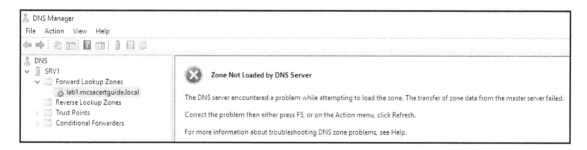

10. This is completely normal behavior as a security feature prevents zone transfers to unknown or unwanted servers.

11. Open **DNS Manager** on a server hosting the primary zone.

12. Right-click on the primary zone and click on **Properties**:

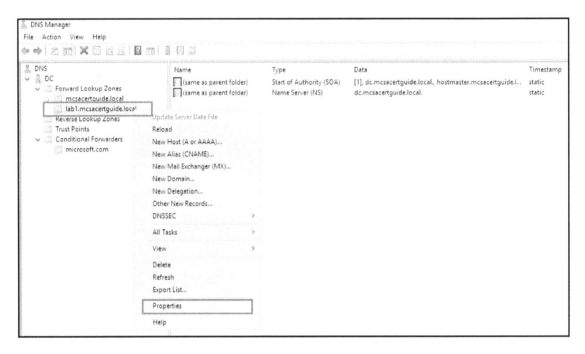

13. The **Properties** page for the zone opens; click on the **Zone Transfers** tab.

14. On the **Zone Transfers** page, you can configure how you want this zone to replicate to other DNS servers. The options are to allow zones to replicate to any server, to the servers listed on the **Name Servers** tab, or to the servers listed on this page:

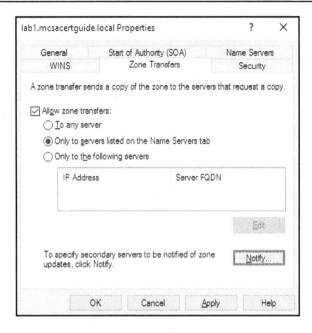

15. In this example, select the **Only to servers listed on the Name Servers** tab, and then click on the **Name Servers** tab.
16. On the **Name Servers** tab, click on **Add...**, type in the FQDN of the server hosting the secondary zone, and click on **Resolve**. Then, click on **OK**:

17. In this example, we added `srv1.mcsacertguide.local` as the server hosting the secondary copy of the `lab1.mcsacertguide.local` zone. Click on **OK** to close the **Properties** window and accept the changes.

18. In the **DNS Manager** window, on the server hosting the secondary zone, right-click on the secondary zone name and click on **Refresh**. If the zone does not load, right-click on the zone name, click on **Reload**, and then click on **Refresh** again. The secondary zone is now available on the DNS server because the server hosting the primary zone was configured to allow the zone transfer to the specified DNS Server:

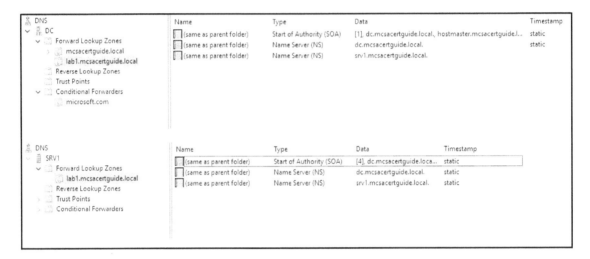

The preceding screenshot shows the primary zone stored on the **DC** computer and the successfully replicated secondary zone on the **SRV1** computer. This is after allowing zone transfers from the DNS servers listed on the **Name Servers** tab, and adding the **SRV1** DNS server as a trusted server on the **Name Servers** tab list.

Summary

In this chapter, we first looked at the requirements and the installation of the DNS server role in Windows Server 2016. Then, we learned how to configure DNS server roles and the different DNS zones. In the next chapter, we will install and configure DHCP server roles.

Configuring DHCP 3

This chapter explains how to install and configure the DHCP server role, create and configure scopes and policies, back up and restore the DHCP server, and achieve high availability.

In this chapter, we will cover the following topics:

- Installing and configuring the DHCP server
- Configuring the DHCP server options
- Managing and maintaining the DHCP server

Installing and configuring the DHCP server

Dynamic Host Configuration Protocol (DHCP) is a TCP/IP standard that facilitates the management of IP addresses and other client configuration options from a centralized location. Windows Server 2016 has a DHCP server role that enables administrators to manage IP addressing and networking configuration with ease, avoiding manual configuration, which minimizes errors, address conflicts, and repetitive tasks. To design highly-available automatic addressing, administrators have used the 80/20 rule, where two DHCP servers shared a scope in an 80:20 ratio. Since Windows Server 2012, the DHCP server role can also be highly available, not by splitting a scope but by enabling two DHCP servers to share a scope.

Installing the DHCP server role

Before installing the DHCP role, like with installing the DNS server role, it is recommended you configure the DHCP server with at least one static IP address.

To install the DHCP server role on a computer running a Windows Server 2016 operating system using Server Manager, complete the following steps:

1. Open Server Manager.
2. From the **Manage** menu, select **Add Roles and Features**.
3. On the **Before you begin** page, click **Next**.
4. Select **Role-based or feature-based installation**. Click **Next**.
5. On the **Select destination server** page, select the current server or a remote server from the server pool and click **Next**.
6. On the **Select server roles** page, select the **DHCP Server** role. When the Add Roles and Feature Wizard page appears, click **Add Features** to add the features required for the DHCP server role. Click **Next**.
7. On the **Select features** page, click **Next**. You already accepted the required features in the previous step. Click **Next**.
8. On the **DHCP Server** page, read the information. Click **Next**:

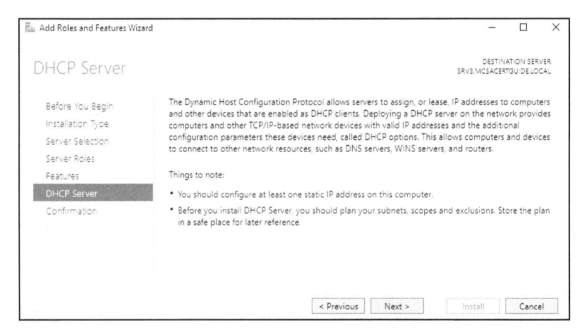

9. On the **Confirm installation selections** page, click **Install**.
10. When the installation finishes, review the results and click **Close**. The DHCP server role feature is installed:

 Although the installation completed successfully, you need to complete additional DHCP server configurations for a DHCP role to be functional.

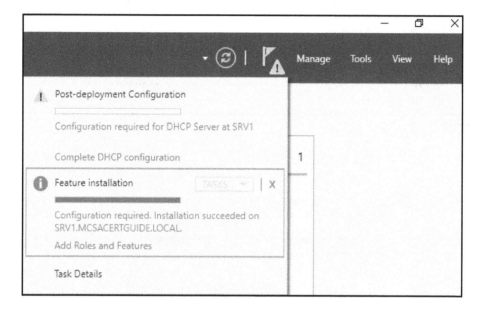

To install the DHCP server role and relevant management tools using PowerShell, use the `Add-WindowsFeature DHCP -IncludeManagementTools` cmdlet.

DHCP Post-Install configuration

After installing the DHCP server role, a few additional steps are required to make the new DHCP server fully functional and able to lease addresses and configuration options to clients.

The Wizard will create the DHCP Administrators and DHCP Users groups and then authorize the DHCP server in the Active Directory, if an Active Directory is present on the network. The authorization creates a server object in an Active Directory, enabling it to operate and lease addresses. After installing and configuring a DHCP server role, a DHCP server will check whether it has been authorized in an Active Directory. If it has been authorized, it will become operational and lease addresses. If it has not been authorized, the DHCP role will not be functional.

To complete the post-installation configuration, follow these steps:

1. Open Server Manager.
2. Click on the flag adjacent to yellow triangle on the top of the window, then click on **Complete DHCP configuration**.
3. The **DHCP Post-Install configuration** wizard opens:

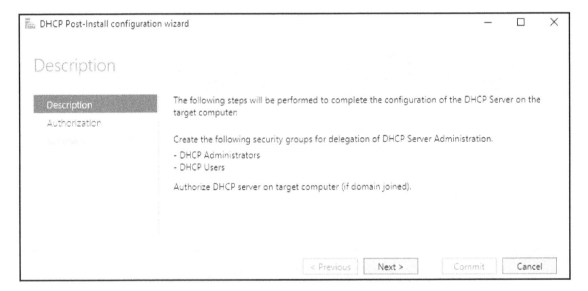

4. Read the information on **Description** page and click **Next**.
5. On the **Authorization** page, specify the credentials to be used to authorize the current DHCP server in the Active Directory Domain Services server. You can use alternate credentials or skip the Active Directory authorization. If you skip the AD authorization, you will need to authorize the DHCP server manually later:

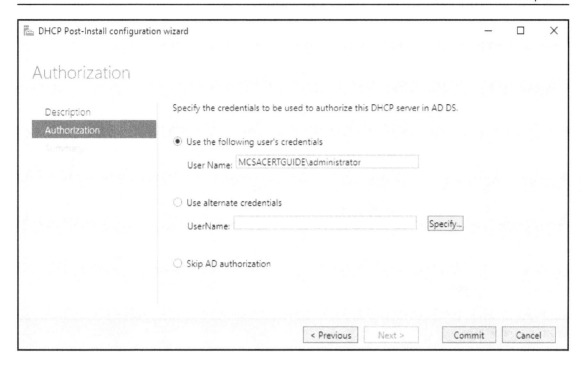

6. Click **Commit** to display the **Summary** page and the configuration steps' status:

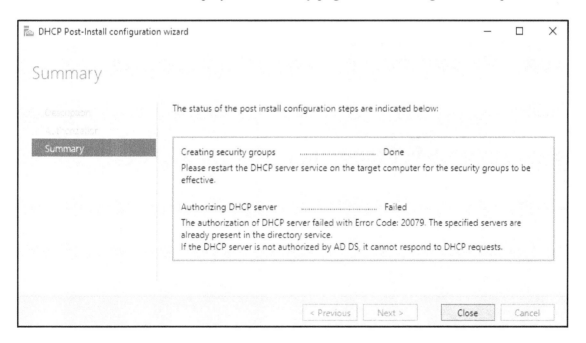

7. When the configuration is completed, click **Close**.

Creating and configuring scopes

To understand the DHCP server role, configuration options, and how to configure and administer DHCP server, you need to be familiar with DHCP server terms.

DHCP server

A DHCP server is a server running the DHCP server role and has information about network configuration, as well as available, leased, and reserved IP addresses, and other network configuration options.

DHCP client

A DHCP client is any computer that acquired IP-address and IP-configuration information from a DHCP server.

Scope

A scope is a contiguous range or a collection of IP addresses that is available for lease to DHCP clients. Each scope has a set of parameters or scope options that is an additional information available for client network configuration.

Lease

A lease is a specific length of time for which a DCHP client can use an IP address that has been obtained from a DHCP server.

Exclusion range

This is a range of IP addresses or an IP address from the DHCP scope or pool not included for distribution or lease to DHCP clients.

Reservation

This is an IP address exclusively reserved for lease to a specific DHCP client.

Creating a scope

To create a scope, complete the following steps:

1. Open Server Manager, click on the **Tools** menu, and click on **DHCP**. Alternatively, open the Start menu, expand **Windows Administrative Tools**, and click **DHCP**.
2. The DHCP console opens. After a DHCP server has been authorized, the green checkmark signs on **IPv4** and **IPv6** configuration options indicate that a DHCP server is healthy and functional. Before a DHCP server can lease addresses, we have to create a scope:

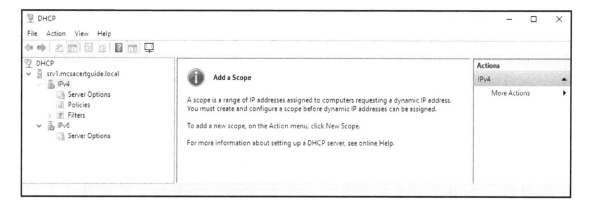

3. To create an IPv4 scope, in the left pane, right-click on the IPv4 node and click **New Scope...** then a **New Scope Wizard** starts. Click **Next**:

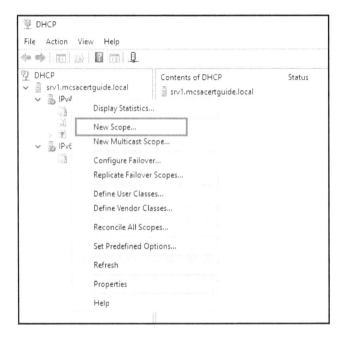

4. On the New Scope page, enter the scope name and description. Adding a good description of the scope is good practice. Click **Next**:

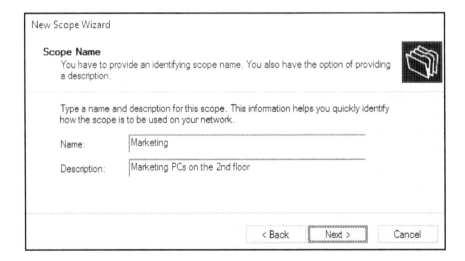

5. At **IP Address Range**, enter the **Start IP address** and **End IP address** that the scope will lease to the clients. As you enter the IP address, the subnet mask is automatically entered, but you can subnet or adjust the subnet mask as needed. Click **Next**:

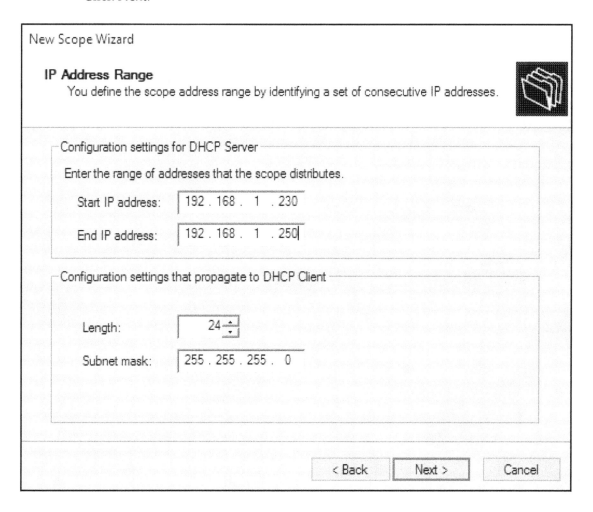

6. On the **Add Exclusions and Delay** page, enter a single IP address or a range of IP addresses that will be excluded from the distribution to clients. To adjust the delay at which the DHCP server responds to client requests, adjust the **Subnet delay in milli second** option. If you do not want to add exclusions now, click **Next**:

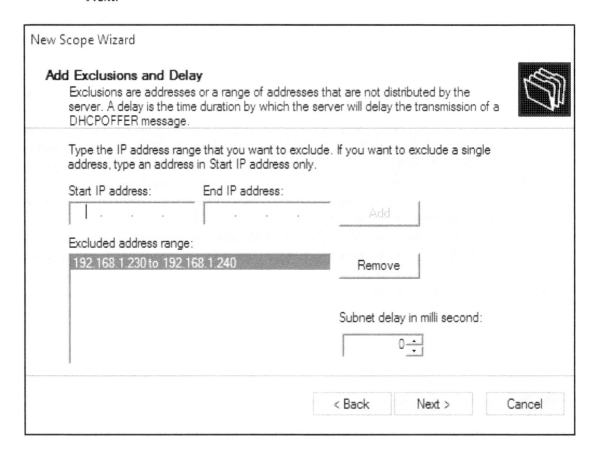

7. On the **Lease Duration** page, specify the lease duration, or the time that a client will be allowed to use the allocated IP address before it expires. After a lease expires, the client needs to repeat the request for the IP address lease. Typically, a lease duration should be proportional to a client's existence on a network. In a dynamic environment, a lease duration should be short:

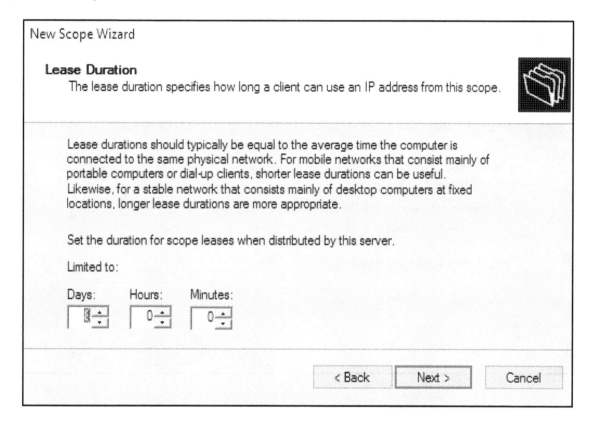

8. On the **Configure DHCP Options** page, you can configure additional DHCP options or finish the scope configuration. Select **Yes, I want to configure these options now** and then click **Next**:

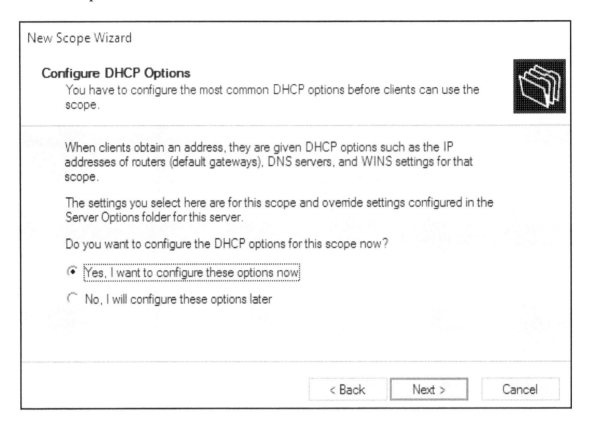

New Scope Wizard

Configure DHCP Options
You have to configure the most common DHCP options before clients can use the scope.

When clients obtain an address, they are given DHCP options such as the IP addresses of routers (default gateways), DNS servers, and WINS settings for that scope.

The settings you select here are for this scope and override settings configured in the Server Options folder for this server.

Do you want to configure the DHCP options for this scope now?

⦿ Yes, I want to configure these options now

○ No, I will configure these options later

[< Back] [Next >] [Cancel]

9. On the **Router (Default Gateway)** page, add the IP address of the router the clients will use to reach outside the subnet. Click **Next**:

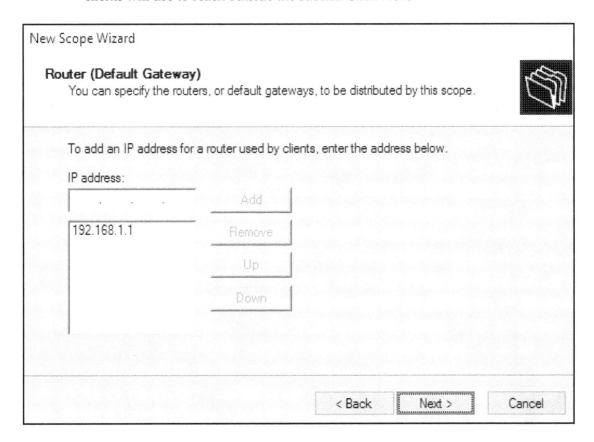

10. On the **Domain Name and DNS Servers** page, enter the **Parent domain** name and the IP addresses or FQDNs of the DNS servers on the network that the DHCP clients will use for name resolution requests. Click **Next**:

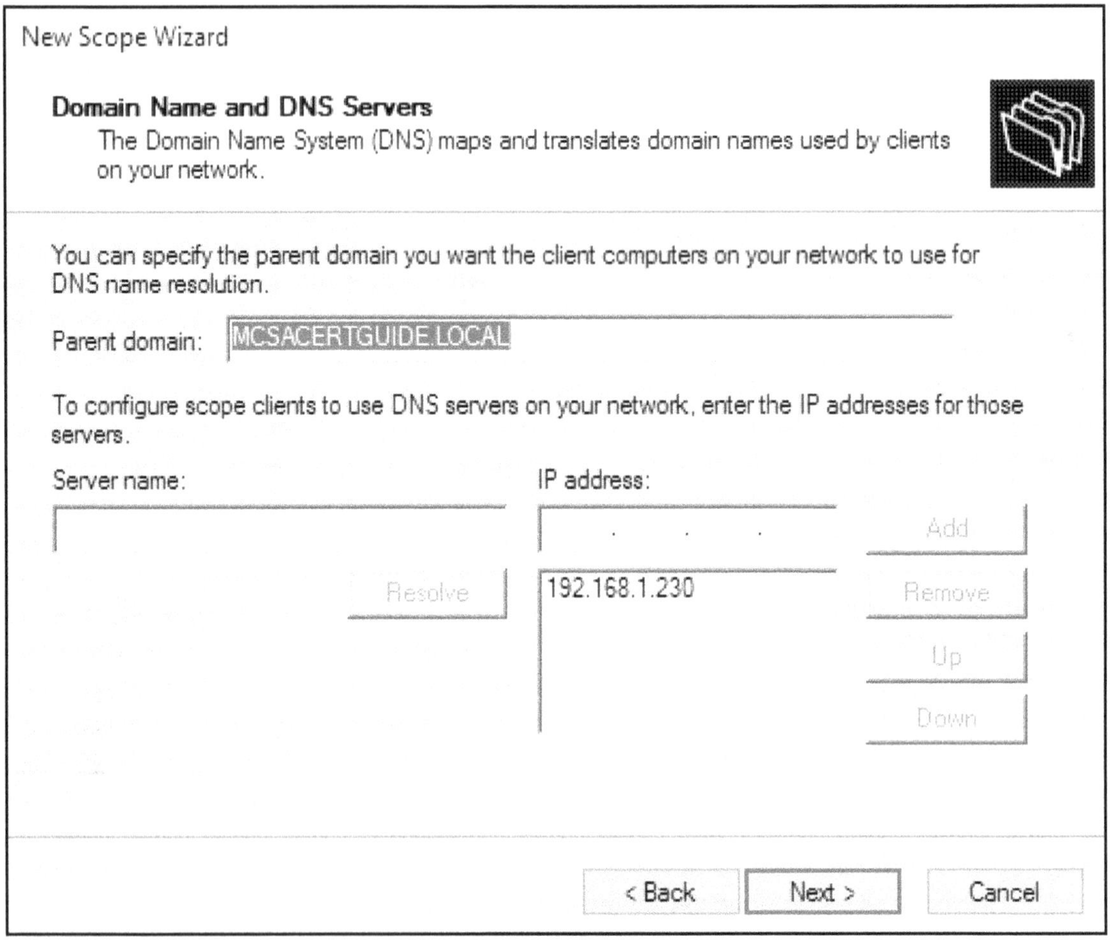

New Scope Wizard

Domain Name and DNS Servers
   The Domain Name System (DNS) maps and translates domain names used by clients on your network.

You can specify the parent domain you want the client computers on your network to use for DNS name resolution.

Parent domain: MCSACERTGUIDE.LOCAL

To configure scope clients to use DNS servers on your network, enter the IP addresses for those servers.

Server name: IP address:

                                                                          Add

                               Resolve   192.168.1.230   Remove

                                                                          Up

                                                                          Down

                                              < Back   Next >   Cancel

---

11. On the **WINS Servers** page, enter the IP addresses or FQDNs of the WINS servers for the DHCP clients to use. Click **Next**:

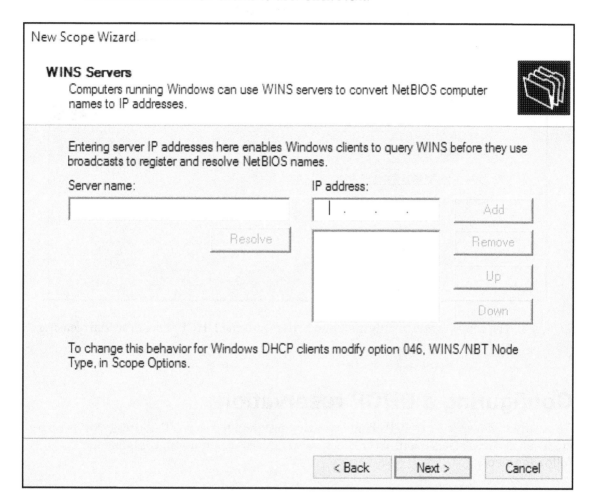

12. On the **Activate Scope** page, you have the option to either make the scope active after the wizard finishes or to finish the wizard and create the scope but leave it deactivated. Activate the scope and click **Next**:

13. The scope is now configured and active, and the DHCP server can start leasing addresses.

Configuring a DHCP reservation

To ensure that a specific DHCP client is always assigned the same IP address, you need to create an address reservation. To create an IPv4 address reservation, complete the following steps:

1. Open DHCP Manager.
2. In the left pane, right-click on **Reservations** and click **New Reservation...**
3. In the **New Reservation** window, add the following information:
   - **Reservation name**: Enter a name for the reservations.
   - **IP address**: An IP address to reserve for the client.
   - **MAC address**: A **Media Access Control** (**MAC**) physical **Network Interface Card** (**NIC**) address of a DHCP client.
   - A description of a reservation for the future reference and ease of administration.

- Type of reservation: Default value is **Both**:

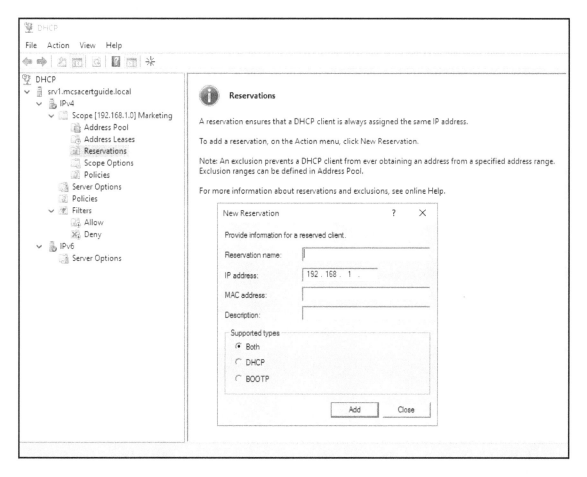

4. Click **Add** and then repeat *steps 1-3* to add additional reservations. When you are finished adding reservations, click **Close**.

Configuring the DHCP server options

The DHCP options are other configuration parameters that a DHCP server can assign to DHCP clients. The DHCP options can be configured at different levels, and the most specific options take precedence over the more general options.

Here are the DHCP options:

- **Server options**: These options apply globally.
- **Scope options**: These options apply to clients that have obtained an IP address lease from a scope.
- **Class options**: These options apply to a client with a specific DHCP Class ID value.
- **Reserved client options**: These options apply to the clients with reservation leases.

The following screenshot shows the DHCP scope options configuration, specifically the router (gateway) options:

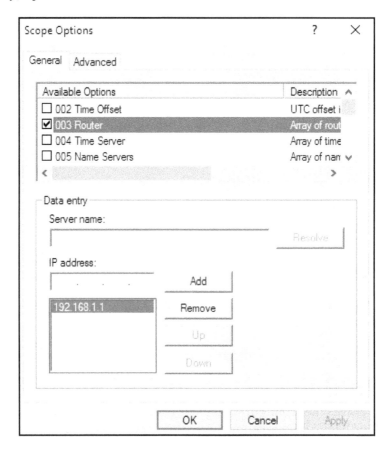

Clients can obtain different types of configuration information through the DHCP options. Some of the common configuration options are as follows:

- **003 Router**: The address of the subnet default gateway router IP address
- **006 DNS Servers**: The address of the DNS servers for name resolution
- **015 DNS Domain Name**: The client DNS suffix
- **044 WINS/NBNS Servers**: The address of the WINS/NetBIOS servers for NetBIOS resolution

Managing scope options

To manage the existing scope, right-click on the scope name and click **Properties**. On the **General** tab, the fundamental scope options are available, such as the IP address range and lease duration:

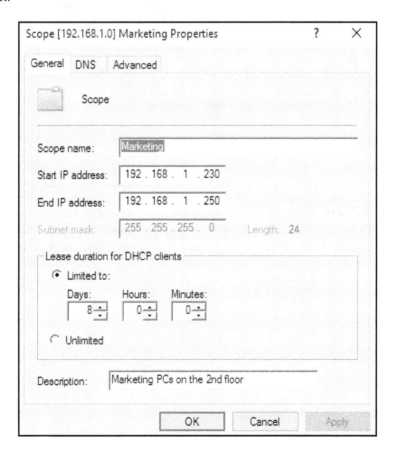

The **DNS** tab has additional configuration options, such as the option to allow DHCP server to update DNS resource records on behalf of a DHCP client, both for forward-lookup zones and reverse-lookup zones, as well as to configure the DHCP name-protection feature:

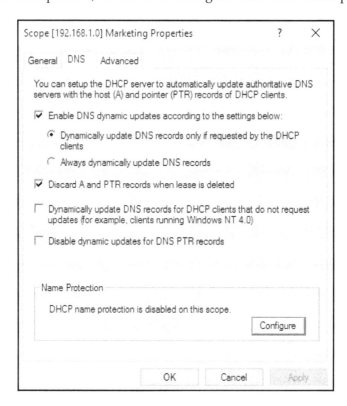

The **Advanced** tab has the options to configure the assignment of IP addresses to **DHCP** clients, **BOOTP** clients, or **Both** types of clients. Further, the delay with which the DHCP server distributes addresses to DHCP clients can also be specified, in milliseconds:

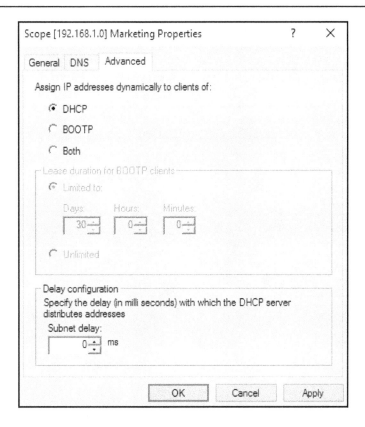

Managing and maintaining the DHCP server

Once you have set up an operating DHCP server, it is common to maintain the server and monitor its performance. Some of the common actions are backing up and restoring the DHCP server, monitoring statistics and performance, and configuring DHCP high availability.

DHCP server statistics

To monitor and view DHCP server statistics, open the DHCP management console, right-click on an **IPv4** or **IPv6** node, and click **Display Statistics...**:

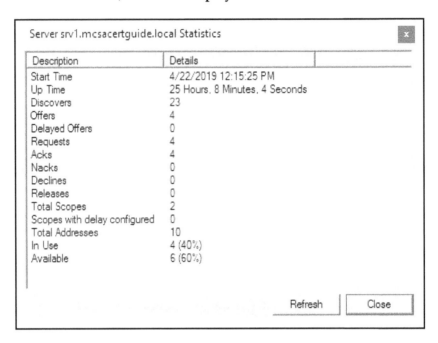

It will open the statistics window for the IPv4 or IPv6 DHCP leases and display information about server performance, scope usage, uptime, and other stats.

Backing up and restoring the DHCP database

The DHCP server stores its configuration and lease data in the DHCP database. The corruption of the database or database files might lead to a DHCP server malfunction and an inability to lease IP addresses to DHCP clients. Thus, maintaining the backup of the database is very important, as well as the ability to restore the database on the same or a different DHCP server. The database is not a single file, but several files stored in the `%systemroot%\System32\dhcp` folder.

The following screenshot shows the DHCP database location and collection of files:

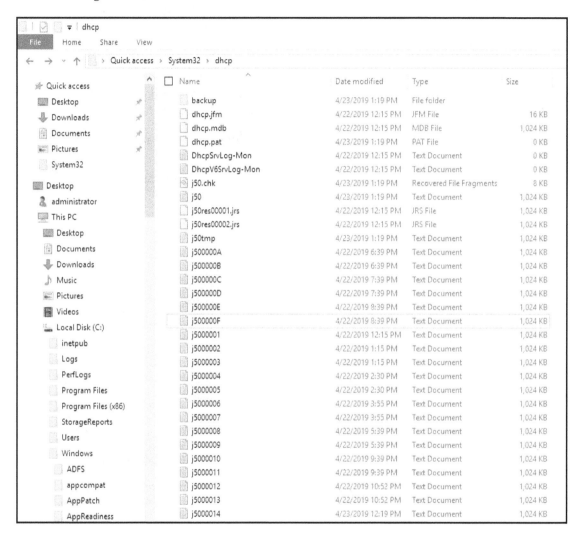

The DHCP database consists of the following files:

- **mdb**: This file is the main DHCP database file
- **log**: This file is the database transaction log that stores the changes to the database
- **j5*.log**: These files are previous transaction logs

- **chk**: This is the checkpoint file used in the database-integrity check
- **jrs, j50res0002.jrs**: These files are database logs used to store uncommitted transactions when the server runs out of the space
- **edb**: This is the temporary database file

The DHCP database backup process backs up the entire database folder. To perform the backup, open the DHCP console, right-click on the DHCP server, and click **Backup**. The same procedure is used to restore the DHCP database if you choose the Restore option.

The following screenshot shows the default backup folder, and you can choose a different backup location:

Configuring split scopes

Achieving DHCP high availability using the split scope method has been known for a long time. A manual split-scope configuration process consists of the following steps:

1. Configure an IP address range for lease
2. Split the scope in an 80:20 ratio

3. Create a scope on the first DHCP server
4. Create a 20% exclusion range on the first DHCP server
5. Create a scope on the second DHCP server
6. Create an 80% exclusion range on a second DHCP server
7. Activate the scopes on both DHCP servers

The Windows Server 2016 DHCP server role has simplified the split-scope creation process significantly. To create a split-scope DHCP server configuration, complete the following steps:

1. Install the DHCP server role on two computers.
2. On the first DHCP server, open the DHCP console.
3. Create a scope. Refer to the information at the beginning of a chapter to do so.
4. On the left pane, right-click the scope, click **Advanced**, and click **Split-Scope**:

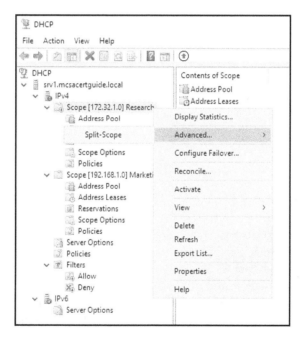

5. The **DHCP Split-Scope Configuration Wizard** starts. Review the information on the first page and click **Next**.
6. At the **Additional DHCP Server** page, click **Add Server** to add a second server to a split-scope configuration.

7. Select a DHCP server from the Active Directory or choose a server from the list of authorized servers. Click **OK**:

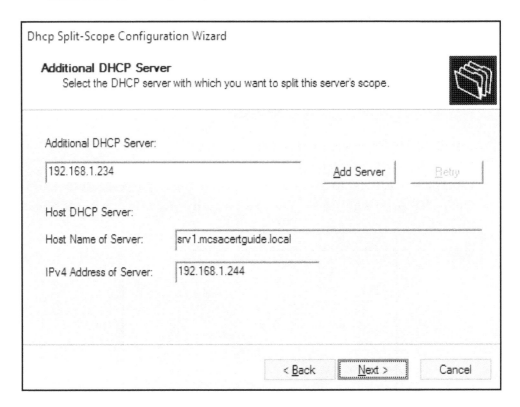

8. The information about the host DHCP server is available on the page as well as the IP address of the chosen secondary DHCP server. Click **Next**.

9. Allow a few seconds for the wizard to contact the second DHCP server. The **Percentage of Split** page shows. Move the slider to choose the percentage of the split between the host DHCP server and the second DHCP server. You can also enter the percentage manually or specify the exclusion IP ranges on each DHCP server. The best practice for creating scopes and limiting the IP range available for lease is to specify the full IP address range for the scope and then create an exclusion range. Click **Next**:

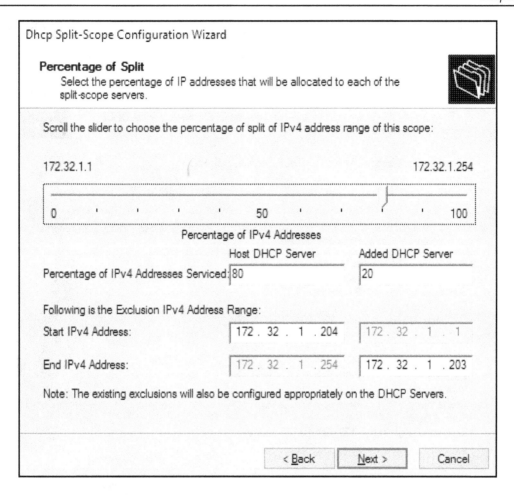

10. On the **Delay in DHCP Offer** page, enter the response delay in milliseconds for both servers to prioritize the distribution of addresses. Click **Next**.

11. On the **Summary** page, review the configuration parameters and click **Finish**:

12. The Split-Scope wizard populates the **Summary** page with the status of the configuration steps. Review the information and click **Close** to close the wizard:

Dhcp Split-Scope Configuration Wizard

Summary of Split-Scope Configuration
Summary of Split-Scope configuration on both the DHCP Servers (Host DHCP Server and Added DHCP Server)

To configure split-scope on both the DHCP Servers, click Finish

Split-Scope is configured successfully. The Scope configured on the Added DHCP Server is in the deactivated state. It needs to be explicitly activated for it to service clients.

Following is a summary of the Split-Scope configuration Wizard's progress, including any errors it encountered while setting up the servers:

Following is the status of the configuration:

Preparation of Host DHCP Server for Scope Migration: Successful
Preparation of Added DHCP Server for Scope Migration: Successful
Scope De-activation on Host DHCP Server: Successful
Configuration of Scope on Added DHCP Server: Successful
Migration of Scope settings on Added DHCP Server: Successful
Configuration of Exclusion Ranges on Host DHCP Server: Successful
Configuration of Exclusion Ranges on Added DHCP Server: Successful
Configuration of Delay in DHCP Offer on Host DHCP Server: Successful
Configuration of Delay in DHCP Offer on Added DHCP Server: Successful
Scope Migration Rollback on Host DHCP Server: Successful

Close   Cancel

The wizard created the scopes and exclusion ranges for us. The following screenshot shows the primary and secondary DHCP servers after completing the Split-Scope wizard and creating split scopes:

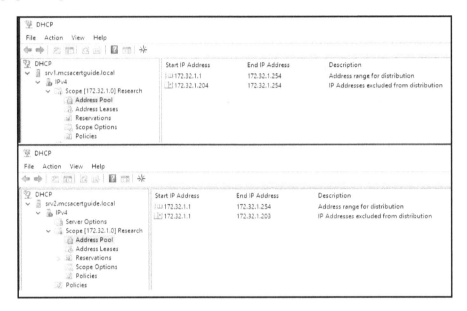

Configuring high availability using DHCP failover

Although the Split-Scope configuration can be treated as a high-availability solution, it has some disadvantages as it does not carry all the benefits of other high-availability solutions, such as clustering or server failover. If the main DHCP server fails, the secondary DHCP server scope might not be big enough to accommodate all the clients' requests for IP addresses.

The DHCP server failover is a high-availability solution that can be set up using two modes:

- **Load-sharing mode**: This mode distributes the load to both DHCP servers at the configured load ratio.
- **Hot Standby mode**. This mode includes the configuration of a primary DHCP server that is in active mode and a secondary DHCP server configured in a standby mode. The primary server leases the IP addresses, while a secondary server takes over only if the primary server fails.

To configure the DHCP Failover, complete the following steps:

1. Open the DHCP console, right-click on the IPv4 (or IPv6) node, and click **Configure Failover...** tab.
2. The **Configure Failover** wizard starts. On the initial screen, select the scopes for which you want to configure failover, or check **Select all** to include all scopes in the configuration. Click **Next**.
3. Specify the partner DHCP server for a failover solution. Click **Next**.
4. On the **Create a new failover relationship** page, the **Relationship Name** field is already pre-populated. Specify the failover mode, either **Load balance** or **Hot standby**. Depending on the mode, some configuration parameters change.
5. The **Load Balance Percentage** configures the percentage of clients each DHCP server will respond to:

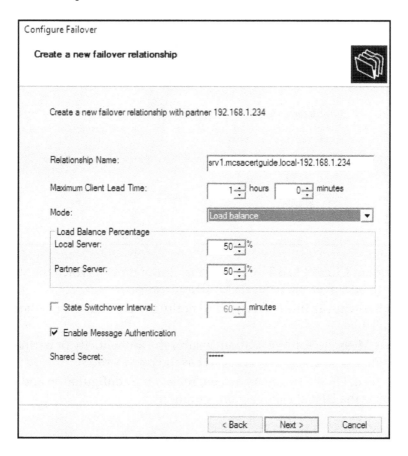

6. For the **Hot standby** mode, configure the **Role of Partner Server** as well as the percentage of the addresses reserved for the standby server:

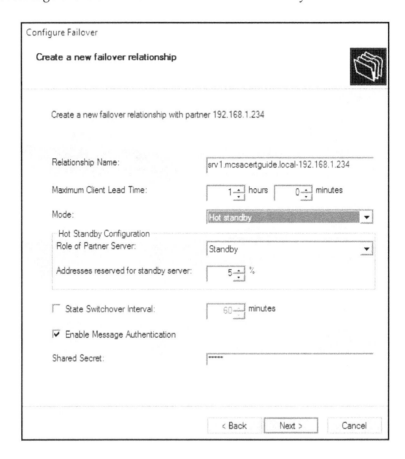

7. **Maximum Client Lead Time** is the maximum time in which the standby server starts to take over the requests for IP addresses.
8. **State Switchover Interval** is used to notify the partner server when other party is unavailable.
9. **Enable Message Authentication** ensures the authenticity of partners' communication using **Shared Secret** as the password.
10. Click **Next**. On the summary screen, review the configuration and click **Finish** to complete the DHCP Failover configuration.

11. A **Configure Failover** status screen appears with the progress information:

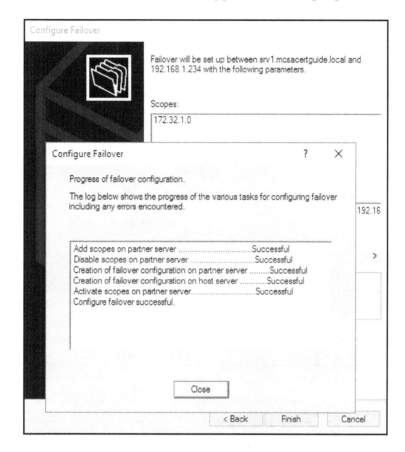

12. Click **Close**.

You can edit and manage the failover configuration after the initial setup:

1. In the DHCP console, right-click on IPv4 and click **Properties**. Click the **Failover** tab
2. On the **Failover** tab, click **Edit** to change the failover configuration parameters
3. To view the information for the scope, right-click the scope, click **Properties**, and click the **Failover** tab

Configuring the DHCP server using PowerShell

You can use the following DHCP PowerShell cmdlets to set up, configure, and manage a DHCP server's IPv4 addressing. The IPv6 PowerShell cmdlets are also available:

Cmdlet	Action
DhcpServer	Back up, recover, export, and import the DHCP server configuration
DhcpServerAuditLog	Manage the DHCP server audit log
DhcpServerDatabase	Manage the DHCP server database
DhcpServerDnsCredential	Configure an account that DHCP server uses to manage DHS server records
DhcpServerInDC	Manage the DHCP server authorization in Active Directory
DhcpServerSecurityGroup	Add security groups to a DHCP server
DhcpServerSetting	Manage the DHCP server database configuration parameters
DhcpServerv4Binding	Manage which network interfaces the DHCP server services are bound to
DhcpServerv4Class	Manage the IPv4 vendor or user classes for the DHCP server service
DhcpServerv4DnsSetting	Configure DNS settings at the scope, reservation, or server level
DhcpServerv4ExclusionRange	Manage the IPv4 exclusion ranges
DhcpServerv4Failover	Configure the IPv4 failover relationships
DhcpServerv4FailoverReplication	Replicate the scope configuration between failover partners
DhcpServerv4FailoverScope	Configure the DHCP IPv4 failover scopes
DhcpServerv4Filter	Manage the DHCP IPv4 MAC address filters
DhcpServerv4FilterList	Manage the filter list status
DhcpServerv4FreeIPAddress	Find free IP addresses in a scope
DhcpServerv4IPRecord	Reconcile inconsistent records in the DHCP database
DhcpServerv4Lease	Manage the IPv4 DHCP leases
DhcpServerv4MulticastExclusionRange	Manage multicast exclusions
DhcpServerv4MulticastLease	Manage the IPv4 multicast lease
DhcpServerVersion	View the DHCP server version information

Understanding IPAM

4

IP Address Management (IPAM) gives a dynamic perspective on your IP foundation, and the view is consistently revived by occasional assignments that keep running on the IPAM server. IPAM additionally empowers directors to play out a few arrangement activities straightforwardly from the IPAM support.

In this chapter, we will cover the following topics:

- Implementing IPAM
- Configuring and managing IPAM
- Monitoring IPAM

Technical requirements

IPAM can be installed using Windows PowerShell, or using the **Add Roles and Features Wizard** in Server Manager. For example, for installing an IPAM server, use the following command at the Windows PowerShell prompt and press *Enter*:

```
Install-WindowsFeature IPAM -IncludeManagementTools
```

Implementing IPAM

IPAM server role in Windows Server 2016 allows you to centralize discovery, management, monitoring, auditing of TCP/IP configuration of your network, greatly reducing errors and administrative burden. It allows you to do so not only with servers running **Dynamic Host Configuration Protocol** (**DHCP**) but with servers running Domain Name Services server role and other infrastructure servers as well.

IPAM servers on Windows Server 2016 provide many advantages:

- Automatic discovery of IP infrastructure servers, DNS servers, DHCP servers and domain controllers on any domain
- Monitor and manage all network and domains DNS and DHCP servers from a centralized place
- Centrally manage and monitor IP address space and IP addresses allocation and utilization
- TCP/IP service management across multiple forests
- Support for /31, /32 subnets in IPv4 and /128 subnet support in IPv6
- Ability to discover free subnets and free IP addresses
- DNS zones and resource records management

IPAM server requirements

A Windows Server 2016 computer running IPAM feature must be an Active Directory member and you can have multiple IPAM servers in a domain and in a forest. An IPAM server feature cannot be installed on a Domain Controller, or on a server running on **Active Directory Domains Services** Server (**AD DS**) role, nor it can be installed on computers hosting DHCP or **Domain Name System** (**DNS**) server role. It is presumed that the IPv4 protocol will be enabled and configured on any networked computer, but in order to use IPAM to manage IPv6 network configuration, scopes and addresses, IPv6 must be enabled on an IPAM server and on DHCP member servers as well.

Generally, it is suggested that IPAM feature is installed on a dedicated server in which case, a virtual server instance will do the job just enough.

An IPAM server will automatically discover DHCP, DNS, and NPS servers installed on Windows Server 2008 versions operating systems and later. It wont detect any non-Microsoft DHCP or DNS servers or network configuration devices though.

To store IP address management configuration data, an IPAM server needs a **Windows Internal Database** (**WID**) or a SQL server.

Installing IPAM Server

The installation of IPAM server is just one of the steps required to set up an IPAM server on the network. The high-level overview of the IPAM implementation are:

1. Install the IPAM server feature
2. Configure the IPAM database
3. Provision the IPAM server
4. Configure the IPAM discovery scope
5. Start network services server discovery
6. Configure settings on IPAM-managed servers
7. Configure managed server's manageability status
8. Verify IPAM access to managed servers
9. Retrieve data from managed servers

To install IPAM server feature, follow these steps:

1. Open Server Manager
2. From **Manage** menu, select **Add Roles and Features**.
3. On **Before you begin** page click **Next**.
4. Select **Role-based or feature-based installation**. Click **Next**.
5. On **Select destination server** page, select the current server or a remote server from the server pool and click **Next**.
6. On the **Select Server Role** page, click **Next**.

7. On the **Select features** page, select **IP Address Management (IPAM) Server**:

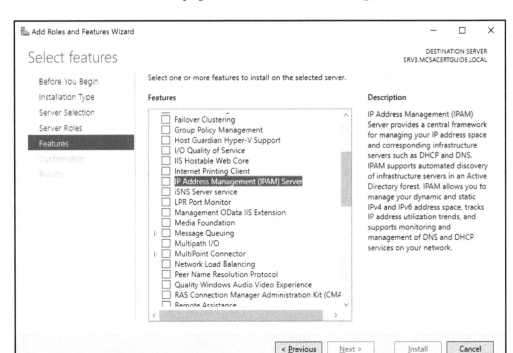

8. When the **Add Roles and Feature Wizard** page appears, click **Add Features** to add features required for IPAM feature. Click **Next** and click **Install** to begin installation and click **Close** to close the installation wizard.

Provisioning IPAM

The process of provisioning IPAM means enabling IPAM server to discover and manage DNS and DHCP servers. When you start IPAM provisioning wizard, few of the provisioning steps are addressed. To start provisioning of IPAM server complete the following steps:

1. Open Server Manager.
2. In the left-hand pane, click **IPAM**.
3. In the IPAM Server Tasks click the task number 2, Provision the IPAM Server.
4. The provision server wizard starts.

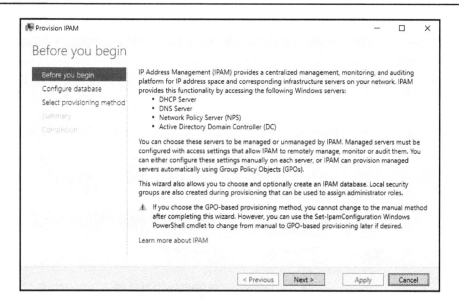

5. Read the information on the page and click **Next**.

6. On the **Configure database** page, select whether to use **Windows Internal Database (WID)** or a **Microsoft SQL Server** instance. Leave the selection on WID and click **Next**.

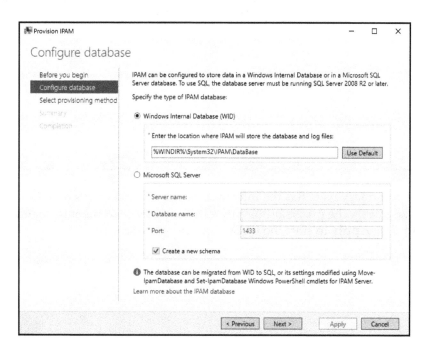

7. On the **Select provisioning method** page, select the IPAM server provisioning method. Two methods are available—**Manual** and **Group Policy Based**. With **Manual** provisioning, you have to manually configure security groups, firewall rules and network shares on each managed server. If you use **Group Policy Based** provisioning method, a required Group Policy will be created with a GPO prefix name you specify. We will use IPAM1 as the GPO name prefix in this example. Click **Next**:

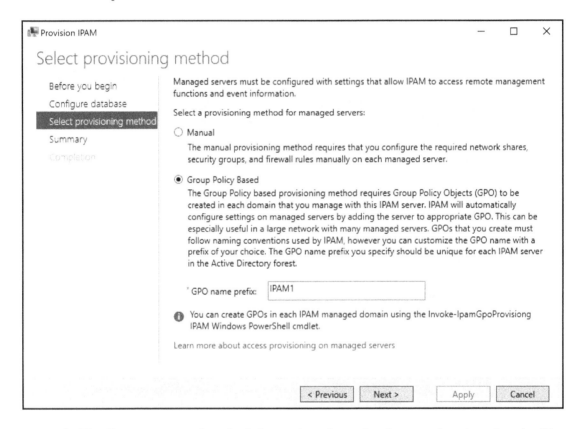

8. The **Summary** page has the information about the changes that the wizard will make during the provisioning process. Carefully read the information provided and click **Apply** to start the IPAM feature provisioning.

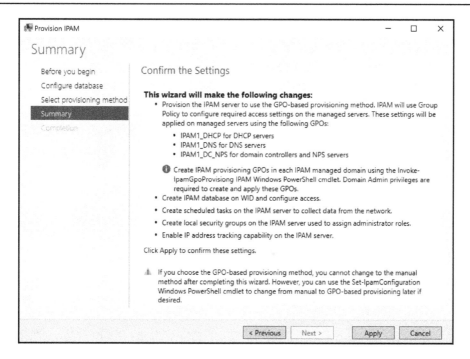

9. When the wizard completes provisioning process, the **Summary** page will show the status of provisioning step's results. Review the information and click **Close**:

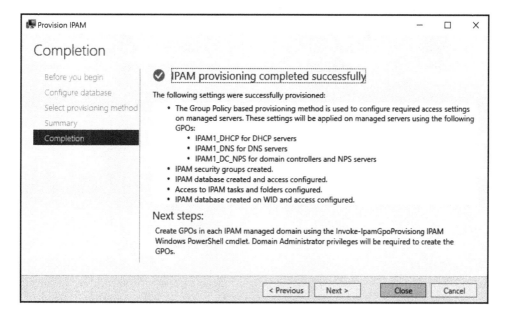

10. Click **Close** to complete and close the wizard.
11. Open PowerShell console.
12. Type in the following PowerShell command. Replace the domain name and the IPAM server FQDN with the values applicable to your network configuration:

```
Invoke-IpamGPOProvisioning -Domain mcsacertguide.local -
GPOPrefixName IPAM1 -IpamServerFqdn srv3.mcsacertguide.local -Force
```

13. If asked, confirm that you want to make the appropriate GPO and domain changes.
14. After the command completes, close the PowerShell window.

Configuring and managing IPAM

Once IPAM server is provisioned you must configure and begin server discovery. Server discovery will initiate search for servers running in specified domains and forests and add them to a management list.

To configure IPAM server Discovery, complete the following steps.

1. Open Server Manager and on the left pane click IPAM.
2. In the IPAM Server tasks click step 3, **Configure server discovery**.
3. The **Configure Server Discovery** window opens
4. Click **Get Forests** button to get the list of available forests. A discovery process starts and you will have to wait for a few moments for a discovery to finish.
5. Close the wizard and click on **Configure server discovery** again to see the list of discovered forests and domains.
6. Click **Add** to add one or more discovered domains to the discover role list.

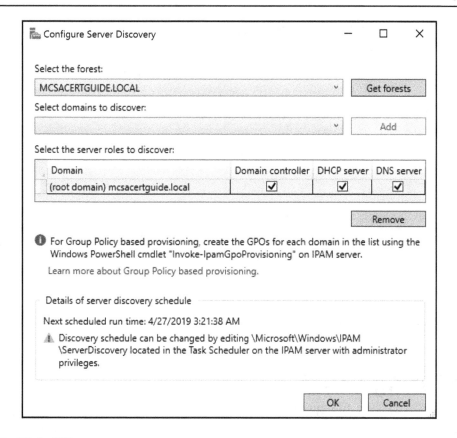

7. Click **OK**.

8. In a Server Manager, click step number 4 – **Start server discovery**.

9. Server discovery starts. While the server discovery is running, a yellow notification bar will inform you to wait for the discovery to complete.

10. Click **More** on the yellow bar to open the information window to see the status of IPAM-related tasks.

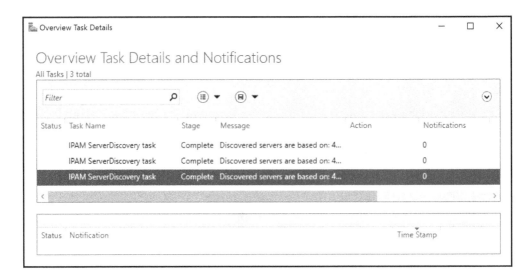

Monitoring IPAM

In Windows Server 2016, IPAM bolsters DNS asset record, restrictive forwarder, and DNS zone the board for both area joined Active Directory-incorporated and document upheld DNS servers. What's more, IPAM underpins job based access control and all usefulness in past forms of the innovation.

This guide incorporates the accompanying areas:

- DNS resource record management
- DNS zone management
- Manage resources in multiple Active Directory forests
- Purge utilization data
- Role-based access control

DNS resource record management

When you send IPAM in Windows Server 2016, you can perform server revelation to add DHCP and DNS servers to the IPAM server the board reassure. The IPAM server at that point progressively gathers DNS information at regular intervals from the DNS servers that it is arranged to oversee. IPAM keeps up a nearby database where it stores this DNS information. IPAM gives you notice of the day and time that the server information was gathered, just as disclosing to you the following day and time when information accumulation from DNS servers will happen.

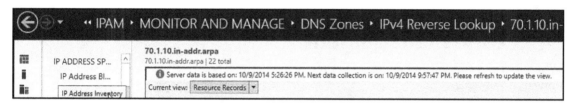

The yellow status bar in the accompanying representation demonstrates the UI area of IPAM warnings.

In Windows Server 2016, IPAM gives joining between IP address stock, DNS zones, and DNS asset records:

- You can utilize IPAM to consequently construct an IP address stock from DNS asset records.
- You can physically make an IP address stock from DNS A and AAAA asset records.
- You can see DNS asset records for a particular DNS zone, and channel the records dependent on sort, IP address, asset record information, and other sifting alternatives.
- IPAM naturally makes a mapping between IP address extents and DNS Reverse Look-up Zones.
- IPAM makes IP addresses for the PTR records that are available in the turn around look-into zone and which are incorporated into that IP address extend. You can likewise physically alter this mapping if necessary.

IPAM enables you to play out the accompanying activities on asset records from the IPAM support.

- Make DNS asset records
- Alter DNS asset records
- Erase DNS asset records
- Make related asset records

IPAM naturally logs all DNS setup changes that you make utilizing the IPAM support.

DNS zone management

When you send IPAM in Windows Server 2016, you can utilize IPAM to oversee DNS zones.

In the IPAM comfort, you can see DNS asset records for a particular DNS zone, and channel the records dependent on sort, IP address, asset record information, and other separating choices. What's more, you can alter DNS asset records for explicit zones.

Manage resources in multiple Active Directory forests

You can utilize this point to figure out how to utilize IPAM to oversee area controllers, DHCP servers, and DNS servers in numerous Active Directory woods.

To utilize IPAM to oversee assets in remote Active Directory timberlands, each backwoods that you need to oversee must have a two path trust with the woods where IPAM is introduced.

To begin the revelation procedure for various Active Directory timberlands, open Server Manager and click **IPAM**. In the IPAM customer reassure, click **Configure server discovery**, and after that click Get timberlands. This starts a foundation task that finds confided in timberlands and their spaces. After the revelation procedure finishes, click **Configure server discovery**, which opens the following dialog box:

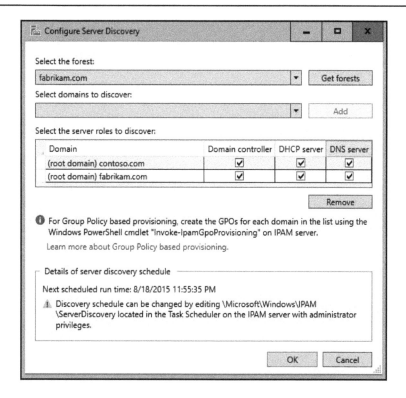

```
Invoke-IpamGpoProvisioning –Domain fabrikam.COM –GpoPrefixName
IPAMSERVER –IpamServerFqdn IPAM.CORP.CONTOSO.COM
```

The DNS servers, domain controllers, and DHCP servers are discovered by default- so if you do not want to discover one of these types of servers, ensure that you deselect the checkbox for that option.

In the example illustration above, the IPAM server is installed in the contoso.com forest, and the root domain of the fabrikam.com forest is added for IPAM management. The selected server roles allow IPAM to discover and manage domain controllers, DHCP servers, and DNS servers in the fabrikam.com root domain and the contoso.com root domain.

After you have specified forests, domains, and server roles, click **OK**. IPAM performs discovery, and when discovery completes, you can manage resources in both the local and remote forest.

Implementing Network Access

5

Today is hard to work in's system condition without experiencing some type of remote access. Regardless of whether it's dialing in from a lodging while on a work excursion or utilizing a virtual private system to associate with the workplace from home, or not withstanding interfacing a branch office by utilizing the Internet and a VPN to interface a branch office, organizations depend on remote access.

In this chapter, we will cover the following topics:

- Implementing **Network Address Translation** (**NAT**)
- Implementing **Virtual Private Network** (**VPN**)
- Implementing **Network Policy Server** (**NPS**)

Technical requirements

You will need three different Windows 2003 servers and at least one remote client for creating a VPN. You need Windows XP up an running on the remote client's machine. The first Windows 2003 server is basically an infrastructure server that should act as a domain controller, DHCP server, DNS server and certificate authority. You do not have to buy a server in case you already have a Windows 2003 network in place.

Implementing NAT

Windows Server 2016 supports a number of technologies to connect to other, remote networks, and for clients to connect to the server, too. In todays world, users expect to be connected to everywhere and everyone, and when reaching for the connectivity, the servers clients are connecting to need to accept the clients' connections in a easy and, most importantly, secure way.

NAT is a IPV4 technology that maps internal, private IPv4 addresses, such as ones on your corporate network, to external, public IPv4 addresses. It enables internal network resources to use internet resources while enabling organizations to use significantly smaller number of IPv4 addresses. This is the main benefit of using IPv4 as the scarcity of IPv4 addresses is increasingly bigger every day.

Windows Server 2016 supports NAT capability along with other network access capabilities as a part of **Remote Access Server (RAS)** role

To configure NAT, you must first install RAS role. Follow these steps to install the RAS role:

1. Open Server Manager.
2. From **Manage** menu, select **Add Roles and Features**.
3. On **Before you Begin** page click **Next**.
4. Select **Role-based or feature-based installation**. Click **Next**.
5. On **Select destination server** page, select the current server or a remote server from the server pool and click **Next**.
6. On the Select Server Roles page, select **Remote Access**. Click **Next**.
7. On the **Select features** page, select **Remote Access Management Tools** node. Click **Next**.
8. When the **Add Roles and Feature Wizard** page appears, click **Add features** to add features required for Remote Access Management Tools feature. Click **Next**.
9. On the **Remote access** page review the information and click **Next**.
10. Select **DirectAccess and VPN (RAS)** and **Routing**. As in the previous step, accept the installation of required features. Click **Next**.

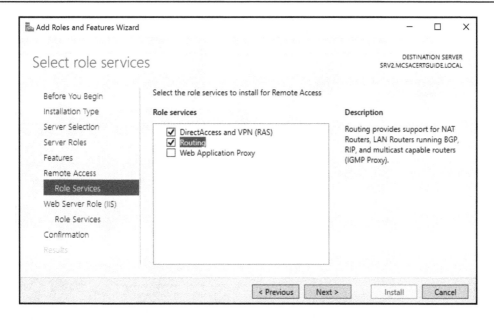

11. Click **Next** two times to accept Web Server Role (IIS) defaults.

12. Click **Install** to begin installation and click **Close** to close the installation wizard when the installation finishes.

13. You will see a **Post-deployment Configuration** screen as shown here:

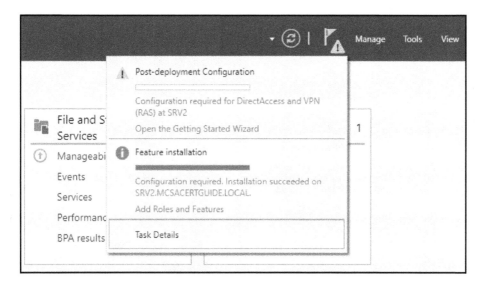

14. Click on **Open the Getting Started Wizard**:

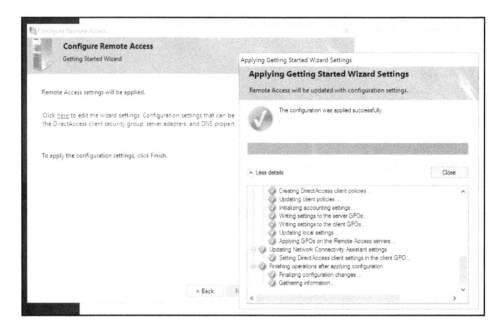

15. Select **Edge** as network topology of the server:

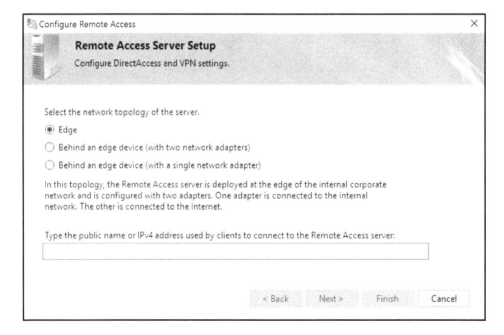

16. Lets try selecting **Behind an edge device (with two network adapters)** and see what it means:

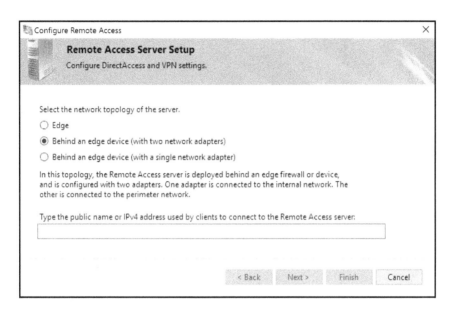

17. In the **Configure Remote Access** window, enter the address required to connect to the **Remote Access server**:

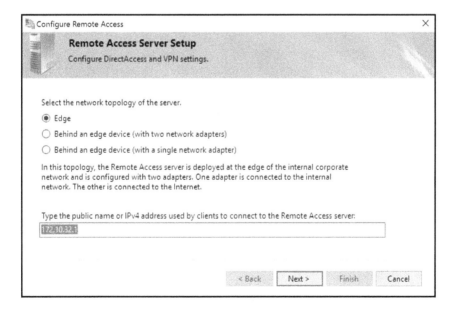

18. Let's explore the **Behind an edge device (with a single network adapter)** option as an topology.

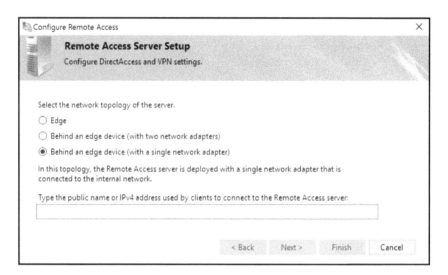

Implementing VPN

Windows Server 2016 supports several VPN technologies—PPTP, L2TP/IPSEC, SSTP and IKEv2. Most of the organizations use L2TP/IPSEC protocol because it is the most secure of these protocols, while the PPTP is the oldest but the most insecure protocols which is not recommended for any serious production use.

Configure Windows Server VPN

1. This is the Routing and Remote Access management console

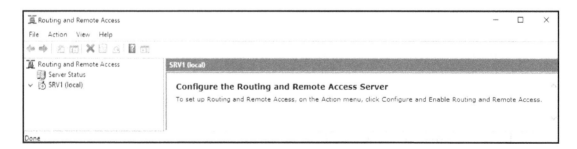

2. Right click on the server name and click on **Configure and Enable Routing and Remote Acces**s.

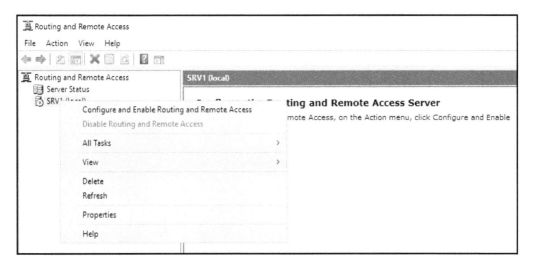

3. On the new wizard, select **Custom configuration** and click **Next**:

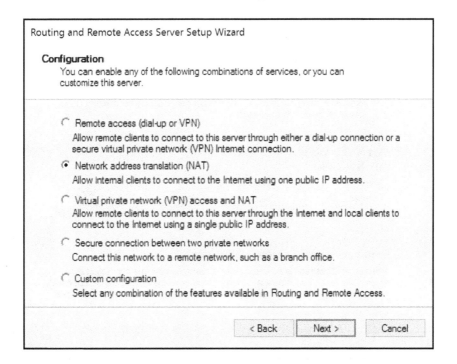

4. Select **VPN access** and click **Next**:

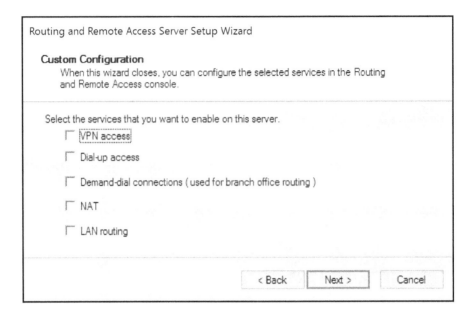

5. Select the DHCP server and click **Next**.

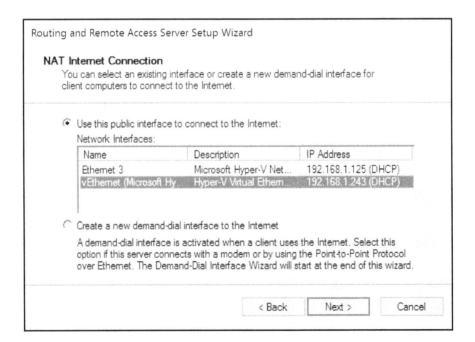

6. After you have click **Finish** you can now start the Routing and Remote Access service.

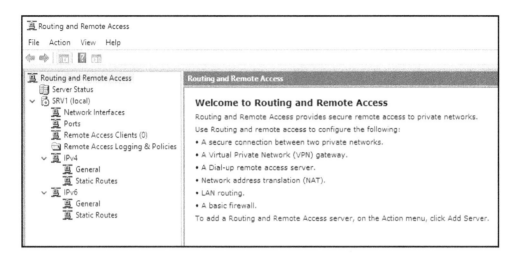

7. Right click on local server and select **Properties**. In **Properties**, select IPv4 Router and click **OK**:

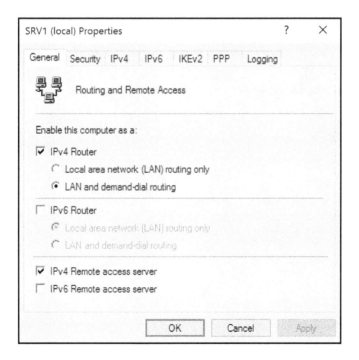

8. Click on **Security** tab and select **Windows Authentication** from the drop down list.

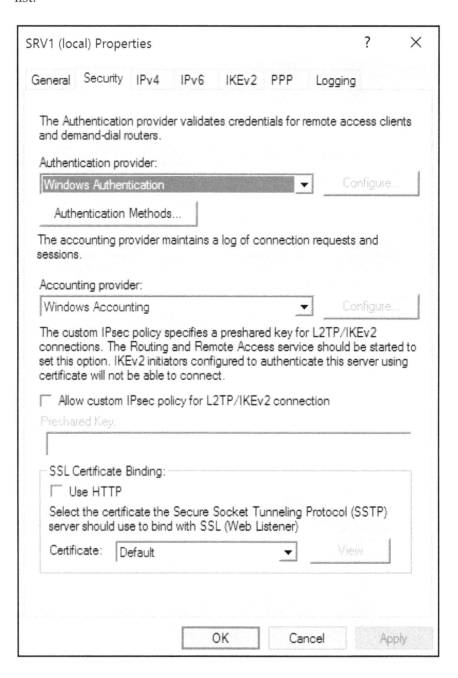

9. In IPv4 tab, select **Dynamic Host Configuration Protocol (DHCP)**.

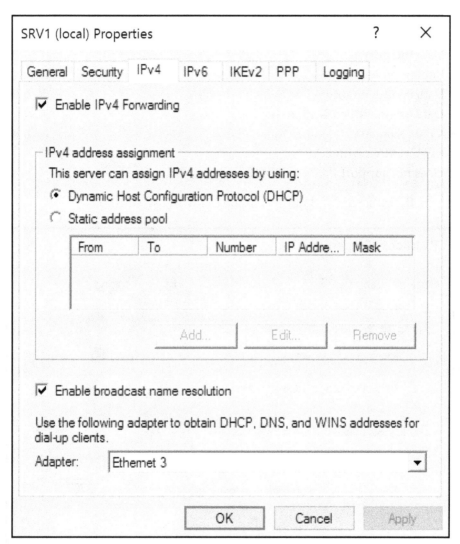

IKEv2 protocol

IKEv2 protocol is a robust protocol featuring reconnection capability without having to authenticate again, even after changing connections, for example, switching from office connection to a mobile internet connection.

IKEv2 protocol features these benefits and characteristics:

- IPv4 and IPv6 protocol support
- Data confidentiality
- Data integrity
- Replay protection
- Data confidentiality
- Data origin authentication
- VPN reconnect
- MS-CHAPv2 with EAP
- Does not support PAP or CHAP

We can see the IKEv2 screen and options in the following screenshot:

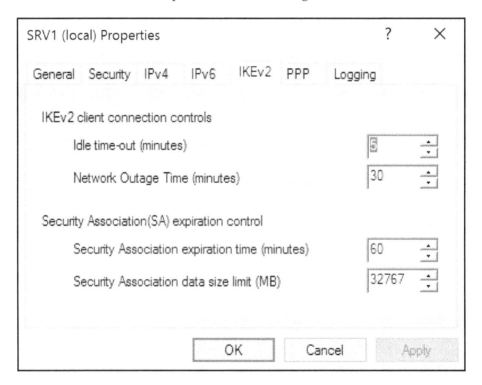

We can modify the Idle time-out and Network outage times.

L2TP/IPSEC

Layer 2 Tunneling Protocol with IPsec has been in use since the early days of Windows 2000 and it is used widely in numerous Microsoft's and others operating systems.

Windows Server 2016 uses several protocols, some of which are more secure, and some are less secure than the others. These protocols are supported in Windows Server 2016, listed from the least secure:

- **Password Authentication Protocol (PAP)**
- **Challenge Handshake Authentication Protocol (CHAP)**
- **Microsoft Challenge Handshake Authentication Protocol version 2 (MS-CHAPv2)**
- **Extensible Authentication Protocol-Transport Level Security (EAP-TLS)**

Here are the steps to configure L2TP and use it as a remote device on your server:

1. Right click on **Ports** and select the **Properties** option:

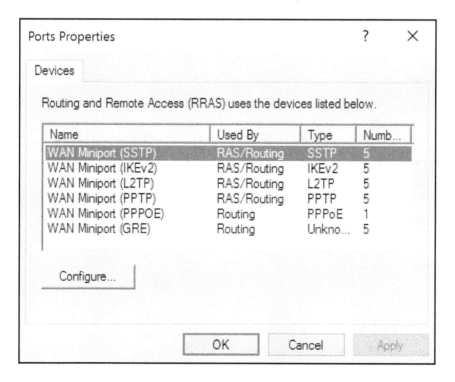

2. Select **WAN Miniport (L2TP)** under the **Devices** section:

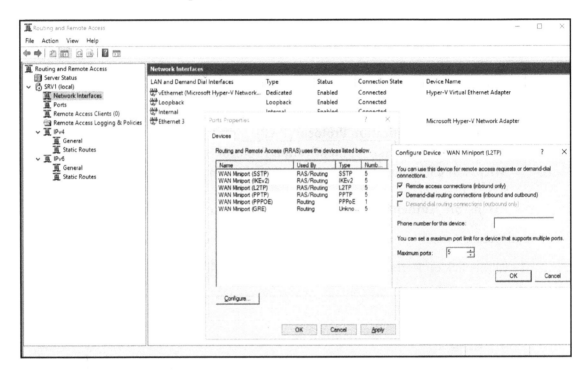

3. We can now configure the port by clicking on **Configure...** button.

Configuring routing protocol

1. In the **Routing and Remote Access** page, select New Routing Protocol... by right clicking on **General** tab

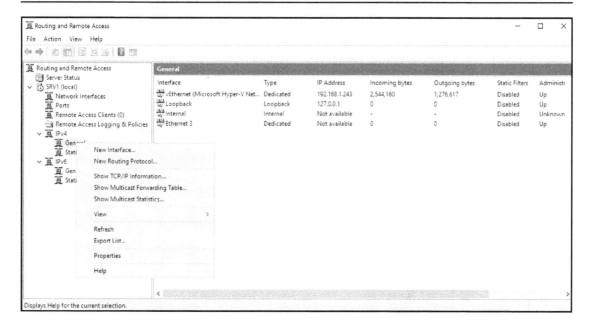

2. In the **New Routing Protocol** setup page, select the routing protocol as **DHCP Relay Agent**.

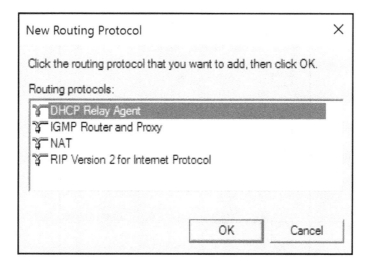

3. You can see the DHCP Relay Agent is configured and can be seen in the IPv4 port.

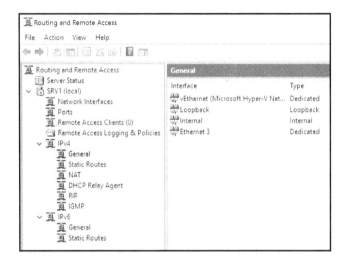

4. Right Click on **RIP** and select **Properties**. Select the **Operation mode** as **Periodic update mode** from the drop down.

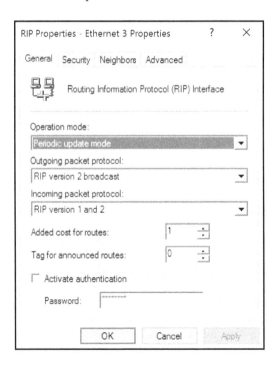

Implementing NPS

NPS is the Microsoft execution of a **Remote Authentication Dial-in User Service** (**RADIUS**) server and intermediary. It is the successor of **Internet Authentication Service** (**IAS**).

As a RADIUS server, NPS performs verification, approval, and representing remote, verifying switch, and remote access dial-up and VPN associations.

NPS is additionally a well being evaluator server for **Network Access Protection** (**NAP**). NPS performs validation and approval of system association endeavors and, in light of designed framework well being arrangements, assesses PC w ell being consistence and decides how to confine a rebellious PC's system access or correspondence. This is another component explicit to NPS just; IAS does not bolster it. See Internet Authentication Service and Network Policy Server for a total rundown of highlights new to NPS.

NPS incorporates two API sets—NPS Extensions API and **Server Data Objects** (**SDO**) API. The two NPS Extensions API and SDO API are likewise bolstered by the forerunner of NPS, the Internet Authentication Service.

NPS Extensions API can be utilized to broaden the confirmation, approval, and bookkeeping techniques offered by NPS and beforehand by IAS.

Server Data Objects API can be utilized to control the system arrangement design on a PC that runs NPS or IAS.

 Note: Network policies in NPS are equivalent to remote access policies in IAS.

NPS Extensions API

The NPS Extensions API is intended for use by software engineers utilizing C/C++ improvement programming. Software engineers ought to be acquainted with systems administration ideas and the RADIUS convention. Span is recorded in RFC 2865 and RFC 2866.

The Server Data Objects API is intended for use by software engineers utilizing C/C++ or Visual Basic advancement programming. Software engineers ought to be comfortable with RAS and the RADIUS convention.

NPS completely bolsters the RADIUS convention. The RADIUS convention is the accepted standard for remote client verification and it is recorded in RFC 2865 and RFC 2866.

Radius authentication and authorization

The accompanying diagram demonstrates a verifying customer ("User") associating with a NAS over a dial-up association, utilizing the **Point-to-Point Protocol** (**PPP**). So as to confirm the User, the NAS contacts a remote server running NPS. The NAS and the NPS server convey utilizing the RADIUS convention.

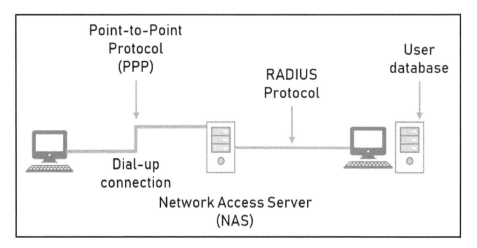

A NAS works as a customer of a server or servers that help the RADIUS convention. Servers that help the RADIUS convention are for the most part alluded to as the RADIUS servers. The RADIUS customer, that is, the NAS, passes data about the User to assigned RADIUS servers, and afterward follows up on the reaction that the servers return. The solicitation sent by the NAS to the RADIUS server so as to confirm the User is by and large called a "confirmation demand."

In the event that a RADIUS server verifies the User effectively, the RADIUS server returns arrangement data to the NAS with the goal that it can give organize administration to the client. This arrangement data is made out of "approvals" and contains, among others, the sort of administration NAS may give to the User (for instance, PPP, or telnet).

While the RADIUS server is preparing the validation demand, it can perform approval capacities, for example, confirming the client's phone number and checking whether the client as of now has a session in advancement. The RADIUS server can decide if the client as of now has a session in advancement by reaching a state server.

6
Understanding Distributed File System

A **Distributed File System** (**DFS**) is a record framework with information put away on a server. The information is gotten to and prepared as though it was put away on the neighborhood customer machine. The DFS makes it advantageous to share data and documents among clients on a system in a controlled and approved way. The server enables the customer clients to share documents and store information simply like they are putting away the data locally. Be that as it may, the servers have full power over the information and give get to control to the customers.

In this chapter, we will cover the following topics:

- Understanding file services
- Understanding DFS
- Understanding BranchCache

Technical requirements

We do not have any additional hardware or software requirements while executing DFS Management or using DFS Namespaces. The name space is hosted by a member controller or a domain controller known as the namespace server. Server Manager can be used in Windows Server 2016 for installing the BranchCache feature for Network Files role service of the File Services server.

Understanding file services

- **File Classification Infrastructure**: You can classify files and apply classification based policies. File classification rules are used to classify the files automatically or manually.
- **File Management related tasks and actions**: Conditional policy or an action can be applied to files based on their classification
- **File screening management**: The user can control the types of files that are stored on a file server
- **Quota Management**: The allowed space for the volume or folder is limited. This space is applied automatically top new folders created on volume.
- **Storage reports**: Identify trends in disk usage and enable data utilization reports

Understanding DFS

- **DFS Namespace**: A centralized folder namespace is provided to the users through which they can access and store files.
- **DFS Replication:** Folder contents are efficiently synchronized between servers and across LAN or WAN network connections.

Requirements for running DFS

The additional hardware or software requirements for running DFS Management or using DFS Namespaces are absent.

Additional consideration before deploying DFS:

- Update the **Active Directory Domain Services** (**AD DS**) schema to include Windows Server 2012, Windows Server 2008 R2, Windows Server 2008, or Windows Server 2003 R2 schema .
- Ensure that all servers in a replication group are located in the same forest. Enabling replication across servers in different forests is not possible.
- Install DFS Replication on all servers members of a replication group.

- Check if your antivirus software is compatible with DFS Replication.
- Folders must be formatted with the NTFS file system if they have to be replicated on volumes. DFS Replication does not support the **Resilient File System** (**ReFS**) or the FAT file system. DFS Replication is also not supported on Cluster Shared Volumes.

Understanding BranchCache

BranchCache is a technology that is used for optimising **wide area network** (**WAN**) bandwidth. BranchCache optimizes WAN bandwidth for remote users that access content on remote servers. It copies content from main office and caches the content at branch office. This way, clients work with the content locally, instead of remotely thus increasing the speed and reducing bandwith and costs.

Locally, content is stored on servers configured as caching host or as distributed cache, on client computers.

BranchCache modes

BranchCache has two methods of activity: circulated reserve mode and facilitated store mode.

When you send BranchCache in appropriated reserve mode, the substance store at a branch office is dispersed among customer PCs.

When you send BranchCache in facilitated reserve mode, the substance store at a branch office is facilitated on at least one server PCs, which are called facilitated store servers.

You can send BranchCache utilizing the two modes, anyway just a single mode can be utilized per branch office. For instance, consider that you have two branch workplaces, one with a server and other without a server. You can convey BranchCache in facilitated store mode in the workplace that contains a server, while sending BranchCache in appropriated reserve mode in the workplace that contains just customer PCs.

In the accompanying representation, BranchCache is sent in the two modes.

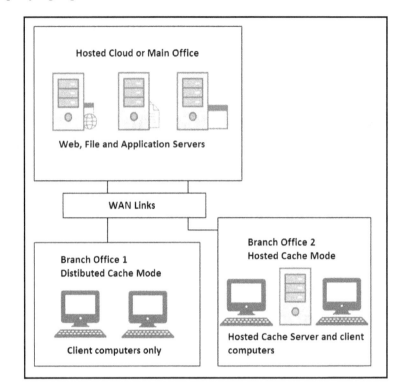

Distributed reserve mode is most appropriate for little branch workplaces that don't contain a nearby server for use as a facilitated store server. Disseminated reserve mode enables you to send BranchCache with no extra equipment in branch workplaces.

On the off chance that the branch office where you need to convey BranchCache contains extra foundation, for example, at least one servers that are running different remaining tasks at hand, sending BranchCache in facilitated store mode is advantageous for the accompanying reasons.

Increased cache accessibility

Facilitated reserve mode expands the store effectiveness since substance is accessible regardless of whether the customer that initially mentioned and stored the information is disconnected. Since the facilitated reserve server is constantly accessible, increasingly content is stored, giving more noteworthy WAN transmission capacity investment funds, and BranchCache proficiency is improved.

Centralized caching for multiple-subnet branch offices

Disseminated reserve mode works on a solitary subnet. At a numerous subnet branch office that is designed for circulated store mode, a document downloaded to one subnet can't be imparted to customer PCs on different subnets.

Along these lines, customers on different subnets, unfit to find that the document has just been downloaded, get the record from the fundamental office content server, utilizing WAN transmission capacity all the while.

When you send facilitated reserve mode, be that as it may, this isn't the situation - all customers in a various subnet branch office can get to a solitary store, which is put away on the facilitated store server, regardless of whether the customers are on various subnets. Also, BranchCache in Windows Server 2016, Windows Server 2012 R2, and Windows Server 2012 gives the capacity to send more than one facilitated reserve server for each branch office.

BranchCache-enabled content servers

When you send BranchCache, the source content is put away on BranchCache-empowered substance servers in your principle office or in a cloud server farm. The accompanying kinds of substance servers are bolstered by BranchCache:

Just source content - that is, content that customer PCs at first acquire from a BranchCache-empowered substance server - is quickened by BranchCache. Content that customer PCs acquire legitimately from different sources, for example, Web servers on the Internet or Windows Update, isn't stored by customer PCs or facilitated reserve servers and after that common with different PCs in the branch office. In the event that you need to quicken Windows Update content, be that as it may, you can introduce a **Windows Server Update Services (WSUS)** application server at your principle office or cloud server farm and design it as a BranchCache content server.

Web servers

Bolstered Web servers incorporate PCs that are running Windows Server 2016, Windows Server 2012 R2, Windows Server 2012, or Windows Server 2008 R2 that have the Web Server (IIS) server job introduced and that utilization **Hypertext Transfer Protocol (HTTP)** or **HTTP Secure (HTTPS)**.

Furthermore, the Web server must have the BranchCache highlight introduced.

Record servers

Bolstered document servers incorporate PCs that are running Windows Server 2016, Windows Server 2012 R2, Windows Server 2012, or Windows Server 2008 R2 that have the File Services server job and the BranchCache for Network Files job administration introduced.

These record servers use **Server Message Block** (**SMB**) to trade data between PCs. After you complete establishment of your document server, you should likewise share organizers and empower hash age for shared envelopes by utilizing Group Policy or Local Computer Policy to empower BranchCache.

Application servers

Bolstered application servers incorporate PCs that are running Windows Server 2016, Windows Server 2012 R2, Windows Server 2012, or Windows Server 2008 R2 with **Background Intelligent Transfer Service** (**BITS**) introduced and empowered.

Likewise, the application server must have the BranchCache include introduced. As instances of utilization servers, you can convey Microsoft WSUS and Microsoft System Center Configuration Manager Branch Distribution Point servers as BranchCache content servers.

BranchCache and the cloud

The cloud can possibly decrease operational costs and accomplish new dimensions of scale, however moving outstanding tasks at hand far from the general population who rely upon them can increment organizing expenses and hurt efficiency. Clients anticipate superior and couldn't care less where their applications and information are facilitated.

BranchCache can improve the execution of arranged applications and diminish transmission capacity utilization with a common store of information. It improves efficiency in branch workplaces and in central command, where laborers are utilizing servers that are sent in the cloud.

Since BranchCache does not require new equipment or system topology transforms, it is a superb answer for improving correspondence between office areas and both open and private mists.

Since some Web intermediaries can't process non-standard Content-Encoding headers, it is suggested that you use BranchCache with HTTPS and not HTTP. For more data about cloud innovations in Windows Server 2016, see **Software Defined Networking (SDN)**.

There are two adaptations of substance data:

- Content data that is perfect with PCs running Windows Server 2008 R2 and Windows 7 is called variant 1, or V1. With V1 BranchCache document division, record portions are bigger than in V2 and are of fixed size. Due to substantial fixed section sizes, when a client rolls out an improvement that alters the document length, not exclusively is the fragment with the change negated, however the majority of the portions as far as possible of the record are discredited. The following require the changed record by another client in the branch office in this manner results in decreased WAN transmission capacity reserve funds in light of the fact that the changed substance and all substance after the change are sent over the WAN connection.

- Content data that is good with PCs running Windows Server 2016, Windows 10, Windows Server 2012 R2, Windows 8.1, Windows Server 2012, and Windows 8 is called form 2, or V2. V2 content data utilizes littler, variable-sized fragments that are increasingly tolerant to changes inside a record. This expands the likelihood that sections from a more seasoned variant of the document can be reused when clients get to a refreshed rendition, making them recover just the changed segment of the record from the substance server, and utilizing less WAN data transfer capacity.

The table found at `https://docs.microsoft.com/en-us/windows-server/networking/branchcache/branchcache` gives data on the substance data form that is utilized relying on which customer, content server, and facilitated store server working frameworks you are utilizing in your BranchCache arrangement.

When you have content servers and facilitated store servers that are running Windows Server 2016, Windows Server 2012 R2, and Windows Server 2012, they utilize the substance data form that is fitting dependent on the working arrangement of the BranchCache customer that demands data.

At the point when PCs running Windows Server 2012 and Windows 8 or later working frameworks demand content, the substance and facilitated store servers use V2 content data; when PCs running Windows Server 2008 R2 and Windows 7 demand substance, the substance and facilitated reserve servers use V1 content data.

When you convey BranchCache in appropriated reserve mode, customers that utilization diverse substance data renditions don't impart substance to one another. For instance, a customer PC running Windows 7 and a customer PC running Windows 10 that are introduced in a similar branch office don't impart substance to one another.

How BranchCache handles content updates in records

At the point when branch office clients alter or update the substance of records, their progressions are composed straightforwardly to the substance server in the principle office without BranchCache's contribution. This is genuine whether the client downloaded the report from the substance server or acquired it from either a facilitated or dispersed reserve in the branch office.

At the point when the changed document is mentioned by an alternate customer in a branch office, the new sections of the record are downloaded from the principle office server and added to the dispersed or facilitated reserve in that branch. Along these lines, branch office clients dependably get the latest renditions of reserved substance.

 You can utilize the table found at `https://docs.microsoft.com/en-us/windows-server/networking/branchcache/branchcache` to decide if to introduce the job administration or the component.

You can install the role service or the feature by selecting the computers where you want to enable BranchCache functionality from Server Manager. In Server Manager, click **Manage**, and then click **Add Roles and Features**. The **Add Roles and Features** wizard opens. As you run the wizard, make the following selections:

- On the wizard page **Select Installation Type**, select **Role-based or Feature-based Installation**.
- On the wizard page **Select Server Roles**, if you are installing a BranchCache-enabled file server, expand **File and Storage Services** and **File and iSCSI Services**, and then select **BranchCache for Network Files**. Select the Data Deduplication role service for saving the disk space and then continue through the wizard to complete the installation. Do not install the **File and Storage Services** role with BranchCache if you do not wish to stall a BranchCache-enabled file server.

- To install a content server that is not a file server or a hosted cache server, you need to select BranchCache on the wizard page **Select features** and then continue with completing the installation. Do not install the **BranchCache** feature in case you do not wish to install a content server other than a file server or a hosted cache server.

BranchCache Security

BranchCache executes a safe by-plan approach that works consistently close by your current system security designs, without the necessity for extra gear or complex extra security arrangement.

BranchCache is non-obtrusive and does not change any Windows verification or approval forms. After you send BranchCache, verification is still performed utilizing area qualifications, and the manner by which approval with Access Control Lists (ACLs) capacities is unaltered. Also, different arrangements keep on working similarly as they did before BranchCache sending.

The BranchCache security model depends on the production of metadata, which appears as a progression of hashes. These hashes are additionally called substance data.

After substance data is made, it is utilized in BranchCache message trades instead of the real information, and it is traded utilizing the upheld conventions (HTTP, HTTPS, and SMB).

Reserved information is kept scrambled and can't be gotten to by customers that don't have consent to get to content from the first source. Customers must be validated and approved by the first substance source before they can recover content metadata, and must have content metadata to get to the reserve in the nearby office.

How BranchCache produces content data

Since substance data is made from different components, the estimation of the substance data is constantly one of a kind. These components are:

- The genuine substance, (for example, Web pages or shared documents) from which the hashes are determined.

- Configuration parameters, for example, the hashing calculation and square size. To create content data, the substance server partitions the substance into sections and afterward subdivides those portions into squares. BranchCache utilizes secure cryptographic hashes to distinguish and check each square and section, supporting the SHA256 hash calculation.
- A server mystery. Every single substance server must be designed with a server mystery, which is a paired estimation of subjective length.

Note: The utilization of a server mystery guarantees that customer PCs are not ready to produce the substance data themselves. This keeps malignant clients from utilizing beast power assaults with BranchCache-empowered customer PCs to figure minor changes in substance crosswise over renditions in circumstances in which the customer approached a past form however does not approach the present adaptation.

Content information details

BranchCache utilizes the server mystery as a key so as to infer a substance explicit hash that is sent to approved customers. Applying a hashing calculation to the joined server mystery and the Hash of Data creates this hash.

This hash is known as the portion mystery. BranchCache utilizes section privileged insights to verify correspondences. Also, BranchCache makes a Block Hash List, which is rundown of hashed information squares, and the Hash of Data, which is produced by hashing the Block Hash List.

The content information includes the following:

- **The Block Hash List**: BlockHashi = Hash(dataBlocki) $1<=i<=n$

- **The Hash of Data (HoD)**: HoD = Hash(BlockHashList)

- **Segment Secret (Kp)**: Kp = HMAC(Ks, HoD)

BranchCache utilizes the Peer Content Caching convention and the Retrieval Framework convention to actualize the procedures that are required to guarantee the protected storing and recovery of information between substance reserves.

Likewise, BranchCache handles content data with a similar level of security that it utilizes when dealing with and transmitting the real substance itself.

7
Advanced Networking Infrastructure

In this virtualization and cloud era, more and more companies want to become cloud providers. One very important task in this process is network virtualization. Slow network connectivity can slow down overall server performance and could damage your business. With Windows Server 2016, Microsoft introduced several high-performance networking features that can enhance network performance in your cloud or datacenter. Another feature, **Software-Defined Networking** (**SDN**), can bypass limitations by using only the physical network, giving you the ability to virtualize your network by adding another layer that is software defined.

In this chapter, we will cover the following topics:

- High-performance networking
- SDN concepts
- SDN network virtualization

High-performance networking

Windows Server 2016 comes with many improvements related to networking. Advanced networking features, such as SMB 3.1.1. or NIC Teaming, are included by default in this version of Windows Server. These features can improve overall performance. In this chapter, we will learn how to deploy and configure advanced networking features in Windows Server 2016.

NIC Teaming and Switch Embedded Teaming (SET)

NIC Teaming is a feature that allows you to combine more than one network adapter in a single network interface, by providing redundancy and/or increasing bandwidth. In Windows Server 2016, you can combine up to 32 network adapters in a single interface. NIC Teaming can be used on a Hyper-V host level, as well as on a virtual machine level. Although NIC Teaming can be used with only one network adapter, in this scenario we cannot provide load balancing or failover. If you want to implement a highly available and fault-tolerant network, you need to use more than one network adapter in NIC Teaming.

NIC Teaming configuration can be done using a Server Manager console or PowerShell commands as follows:

1. Open the **Server Manager** console.
2. Go to the **Local Server** and then click on **NIC Teaming:**

3. Click on **New team** on the drop-down menu.
4. Add the team name, select network adapters, and click on **OK:**

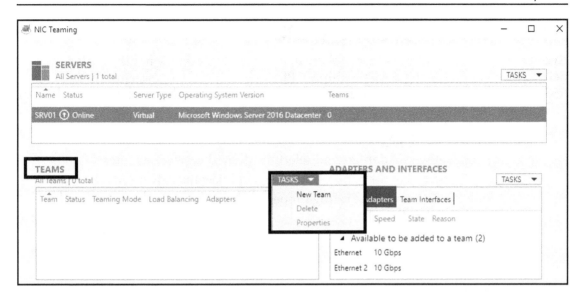

If you want to do this using PowerShell, you need to run the following command:

```
New-NetLbfoTeam -Name <TeamName> -TeamMembers <NetworkAdapterNames>
```

In Windows Server 2016, you can create **Switch Embedded Teaming (SET)**. SET needs to be created within Hyper-V. It gives you the ability to use **Remote Direct Memory Access (RDMA)**-capable network adapters by teaming up to eight physical network adapters to one virtual SDN adapter. This allows you to use RDMA and SET at the same time and utilize network adapters in your server. SET can be created by using the following PowerShell command:

```
New-VMSwitch -Name <SETName> -NetAdapterName <NetworkAdapterNames> -
EnableEmbeddedTeaming $true
```

Receive-Side Scaling (RSS)

Receive-Side Scaling (**RSS**) is a technology that allows for the efficient distribution of network receive processing across multiple CPUs in multiprocessor systems. By default, RSS is enabled on Windows Server 2016, but if you want to disable or re-enable this feature, you can use Device Manager or PowerShell:

1. Open **Device Manager.**
2. Expand **Network Adapters** and select the desired network adapter.
3. Open **Properties** of the network adapter and select the **Advanced** tab.
4. Locate the **Receive Side Scaling** property and define the value as **Enabled** or **Disabled.**

If you want to do this using PowerShell, you need to use the `Disable-NetAdapterRss` or `Enable-NetAdapterRss` cmdlets, as shown in the following command:

```
Disable-NetAdapterRss -Name <AdapterName>

Enable-NetAdapterRss -Name <AdapterName>
```

SMB 3.1.1.

SMB 3.1.1. is the latest version of SMB and was introduced with Windows 10 and Windows Server 2016. It comes with many features, such as SMB Direct and SMB Multichannel, and also requires security negotiations when connecting to SMB 2.x devices. As mentioned in previous chapters, Hyper-V in Windows Server 2016 can use SMB 3.1.1. as a shared storage for Failover Cluster implementation or for Scale-Out File Server implementation.

SMB Direct

SMB Direct supports the use of network adapters that have RDMA capabilities. With RDMA, network adapters can function at full speed with very low latency. That feature is enabled by default in Windows Server 2016 and you don't need to enable it. If you want to disable or re-enable this feature, you need to use the `Enable-NetAdapterRdma` or `Disable-NetAdapterRdma` PowerShell cmdlets via the following command:

```
Disable-NetAdapterRdma <AdapterName>

Enable-NetAdapterRdma <AdapterName>
```

If you want to disable or re-enable this feature on all network adapters, you need to use the `Set-NetOffloadGlobalSetting` PowerShell cmdlet as follows:

```
Set-NetOffloadGlobalSetting -NetworkDirect Disabled

Set-NetOffloadGlobalSetting -NetworkDirect Enabled
```

SMB Multichannel

SMB Multichannel allows file servers to use multiple network connections simultaneously in order to provide high performance and fault tolerance when multiple paths are available between the SMB 3.0 (or later) client and server. This feature is enabled by default to all Windows 10 and Windows Server 2016 operating systems. You can check and enable/disable this feature using the `Get-SmbServerConfiguration` and `Set-SmbServerConfiguration` PowerShell cmdlets:

```
(Get-SmbServerConfiguration).EnableMultiChannel

Set-SmbServerConfiguration -EnableMultiChannel $true
```

Virtual RSS (vRSS)

vRSS allows network adapters to balance network processing loads to all cores that are assigned to virtual machines. Using vRSS, virtual machines can process a greater amount of network traffic. To implement vRSS, the host's CPU must support RSS and the network adapter must support the **Virtual Machine Queue** (**VMQ**).

You can use Device Manager or PowerShell if you want to enable vRSS, by following these steps:

1. Open **Device Manager.**
2. Expand **Network Adapters** and select the desired network adapter.
3. Open **Properties** for the network adapter and select the **Advanced** tab.
4. Locate the **Receive Side Scaling property** and define the value as **Enabled** or **Disabled.**

The following PowerShell command needs to be used if you want to implement vRSS via PowerShell:

```
Enable-NetAdapterRSS -Name <AdapterName>
```

Virtual Machine Multi-Queue and single-root I/O virtualization

Single-root I/O virtualization (**SR-IOV**) allows multiple virtual machines to use the same PCI Express physical hardware resources. This feature requires us to install specific hardware and drivers. Only 64-bit virtual machines from Windows Server 2012 support SR-IOV. SR-IOV uses **Virtual Function** (**VF**), which is associated with Physical Function, which is equivalent to a regular PCI device. A single PCI Express device can expose multiple VFs, such as a multiple-port networking device. By using SR-IOV, a part of the network adapter's hardware is made available to the virtual machine. Because a virtual machine doesn't manipulate physical hardware, you need to install the appropriate drivers.

Virtual Machine Multi-Queue (**VMMQ**) is a new technology in Window Server 2016. VMMQ allows multiple I/O queues on network adapters to map to multiple virtual processor cores on virtual machines instead of VMQ, where a single virtual machine could be allocated a single VMQ. The distribution of traffic between queues is performed by the NIC, avoiding overhead on the CPU. A virtual machine must have multiple cores (vCPUs) to enable VMMQ and each queue should be bound to a specific core.

SDN

SDN allows organizations to manage their networks more dynamically using software layers. With SDN, you can virtualize your network infrastructure and define policies to manage your network traffic. In this section, you will learn about SDN and how to prepare an organization to use SDN.

SDN overview

Although SDN requires a physical network, with SDN you can do the following:

- Virtualize a network layer
- Define policies to manage physical and virtual network flows
- Manage a virtualized network infrastructure

Since Windows Server 2012, Microsoft has implemented SDN with the following components:

- **Network Controller**: Provides centralized management, configuration, monitoring, and troubleshooting for virtual and physical network infrastructures
- **Hyper-V network virtualization**: Abstracts applications and workloads from the underlying physical network using virtual networks
- **Hyper-V Virtual Switch**: Gives you the ability to connect virtual machines to both virtual networks and physical networks
- **Routing and Remote Access Service (RRAS) Multitenant Gateway**: Extends network boundaries to Microsoft Azure
- **NIC Teaming**: Gives you the ability to configure multiple network adapters as a team for bandwidth aggregation and redundancy

SDN benefits and requirements

Generally, SDN offers a lot of benefits for users who have large on-premise infrastructures. Due to limitations of standard on-premise environments, however, some problems can be difficult to solve. Problems commonly faced by customers include the following:

- Resources are not infinite.
- Resources are inflexible.
- Mistakes are expensive.
- Networks are not always secure.

SDN gives you the ability to surpass the limitations of on-premise infrastructures. Your infrastructure, with SDN, can be flexible, efficient, and scalable. Before you can deploy SDN, you must plan all aspects of your infrastructure, and meet all prerequisites. The latter can be separated into two categories:

- **Physical network:**
    - **Virtual Local Area Networks (VLANs)**
    - Routers
    - **Border Gateway Protocol (BGP)** devices
    - **Data Center Bridging (DCB)**
- **Physical compute hosts:**
    - Windows Server 2016
    - Hyper-V role enabled
    - External Hyper-V Virtual Switch

SDN configuration

Once you ensure that your infrastructure has met all the afore mentioned requirements, you can start planning your SDN configuration.

For example, you can have four Hyper-V hosts and two separate tenants, as shown in the following diagram:

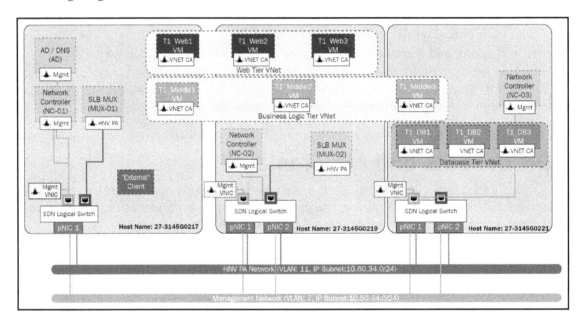

Image source: cloudblogs.microsoft.com

The most common SDN deployments consist of the following components:

- Management logical networks
- Hyper-V network virtualization provider logical networks

 Each physical host must have least one IP address in a management logical network and must be able to access both management and Hyper-V network virtualization provider networks.

- Logical networks for the gateway and the **Software Load Balancer** (SLB)
- A transit logical network for RAS Gateway and SLB Multiplexer

- A public **Virtual IP** (**VIP**) that needs to be routable from the internet and needs to provide external clients with access to virtual networks
- A private VIP that needs to be used for internal access and that doesn't need to be routable
- A **Generic Route Encapsulation** (**GRE**) VIP for the logical network
- Logical networks required for RDMA-based storage
- Routing infrastructure
- Default gateways
- Network hardware

Deploying SDN

Once you finish planning and configuring your SDN, you can start deploying it. In general, deploying SDN has three steps:

1. Install host networking and validate the configuration.
2. Run SDN Express scripts and validate the setup.
3. Deploy a tenant workload and validate the deployment.

The easiest way to deploy SDN is by using scripts. All necessary scripts for SDN are published to GitHub, so you can use the following link to download them: `https://github.com/Microsoft/SDN`.

To install host networking and validate the configuration, perform the following steps:

1. On your compute hosts, install the latest network drivers for all network adapters, install a Hyper-V role, and create a virtual switch for management.
2. Attach the management **virtual NIC** (**vNIC**) to the management virtual switch and configure the defined VLAN for the management logical network.
3. Assign valid IP configuration to the management vNIC.
4. Deploy **Active Directory Domain Services** (**AD DS**) and then join the Hyper-V hosts to the domain.

To run SDN Express scripts and validate the setup, perform the following steps:

1. Download the scripts from the previously mentioned GitHub link.
2. Set up the deployment machine with Windows Server 2016.
3. Extract the scripts and copy the `SDNExpress` folder to the root of the `C:` drive.

4. Share the `C:\SDNExpress` folder.

5. Edit and configure the `FabricConfig.psd1` scripts by replacing the `<<Replace>>` tags to the values of your SDN configuration:

   - The domain name
   - The host names
   - The username and password
   - The network information

6. Create DNS host records for the Network Controller.

7. Run the following script as the domain admin:

   `SDNExpress\scripts\SDNExpress.ps1 —ConfigurationDataFile FabricConfig.psd1 —Verbose`

If you have to roll back the configuration, run the following command:

`SDNExpress\scripts\SDNExpressUndo.ps1 —ConfigurationDataFile FabricConfig.psd1 —Verbose`

To deploy a sample tenant workload and validate the deployment, perform the following steps:

1. Edit and configure `TenantConfig.psd1` by changing the `<< Replace >>` tags with specific values, including the following:

   - The name of the virtual hard disk image
   - Network Controller REST name
   - vSwitch name

2. Run the following script:

   `SDNExpress\scripts\SDNExpressTenant.ps1 —ConfigurationDataFile TenantConfig.psd1 —Verbose`

If you have to roll back the configuration, run the following command:

`SDNExpress\scripts\SDNExpressTenant.ps1 —Undo —ConfigurationDataFile TenantConfig.psd1 —Verbose`

3. Validate the tenant deployment

Due to frequent changes on GitHub repositories, the location of some scripts might be changed and some scripts may be deleted. In order to stay informed, please refer to the following link about deploying SDN: `https://docs.microsoft.com/en-us/windows-server/networking/sdn/deploy/deploy-a-software-defined-network-infrastructure-using-scripts`.

SDN network virtualization

Network virtualization, as a part of SDN in Windows Server 2016, gives you the ability to isolate virtual networks that are on the same physical infrastructure in a similar way that the server isolates virtual machines on Hyper-V. In this section, we will learn about the important components of network virtualization in Windows Server 2016.

The benefits of network virtualization

Just as Hyper-V server provides the functionality to manage multiple virtual machines on the same host and isolate the workload between them, network virtualization allows you to manage network traffic in a similar way. You can have multiple virtual networks on the same physical hardware that are logically isolated. From a virtual network perspective, it will seem as if only one virtual network uses the physical network.

Network virtualization is an important part of SDM implementation, because it provides another layer on top of the physical network. The Hyper-V Virtual Switch in Windows Server 2016 supports network virtualization by using two IP addresses for each virtual machine. With those IP addresses, you can use network virtualization to keep the virtualized logical network topology separated from the actual underlying physical network topology.

As a layer of abstraction between virtual and physical network, network virtualization provides the following benefits:

- **Flexible virtual machine placement**: The IP address or VLAN isolation on the physical network layer no longer means you have to place the virtual machine in a datacenter. You can place a virtual machine on any Hyper-V host.
- **Multitenant network isolation without VLANs**: Network virtualization uses a 24-bit identifier instead of a 12-bit identifier for VLANs. Because of this, you are not limited to 4,094 VLAN IDs per one physical network.

- **IP address reuse**: Virtual networks are isolated and can use the same address spaces without any conflict. This gives you the ability to deploy more than one virtual network with overlapped IP address space on the same physical network.

- **Live migration across subnets**: Virtual machine live migration is limited to the same IP subnet. Live migration between different subnets is not possible because the IP address of the virtual machine needs to be changed to match the new network. With network virtualization, you can perform live migration of virtual machines between different Hyper-V hosts without changing the IP address. The virtual machine location will be changed, updated, and synchronized between all other hosts and computers.

- **Compatibility with existing network infrastructure**: You don't need to redesign the physical network in the datacenter to implement network virtualization. Network virtualization is compatible with the existing infrastructure.

- **Transparently moving virtual machines to IaaS**: In most scenarios, virtual machines that are hosted to network virtualized datacenters are accessible through the internet. You can move virtual machines between Hyper-V hosts in your datacenter, a different datacenter, or to Azure or another public cloud.

- **Support for resource metering**: Just as we can use resource metering for virtual machines on a single Hyper-V host, we can also enable network resource metering for virtual machines that use network virtualization.

- **Configuration using Windows PowerShell**: Network virtualization supports configuring network virtualization and isolation policies via Windows PowerShell.

Network Virtualization using Generic Routing Encapsulation

Windows Server 2016 Hyper-V uses **Network Virtualization using Generic Routing Encapsulation** (**NVGRE**) to implement network virtualization. As mentioned earlier, each virtual network adapter in network virtualization is associated with two IP addresses:

- **The Customer Address (CA)**: The IP address is configured in the properties of the virtual machine virtual network adapter and used by the virtual machine, regardless of whether or not it uses network virtualization. Virtual machines use the customer address to communicate with other systems. The CA IP address will remain the same if you move the virtual machine to a different Hyper-V host.

- **The Provider Address (PA)**: In network virtualization, a PA will be assigned to a Hyper-V host and is dependent on the physical network infrastructure where Hyper-V is connected. All packets that are sent over the network by the virtual machine will be encapsulated and include a PA as a source address. The PA is only visible on physical networks and not on virtual machines. The PA will be changed if you migrate your virtual machine to a different Hyper-V host.

As mentioned, when a virtual machine communicates over the network, the NVGRE will encapsulate packets. In a scenario in which you have two virtual machines on two different Hyper-V hosts, the following IP addresses are configured:

- Hyper-V host 1 192.168.100.10 (PA 1)
- Hyper-V host 2 192.168.100.20 (PA 2)
- Virtual machine 1 10.10.1.111 (CA 1)
- Virtual machine 2 10.10.1.222 (CA 2)

The following diagram provides a simple schematic showing of virtual machines, Hyper-V hosts, and their IP addresses in SDN:

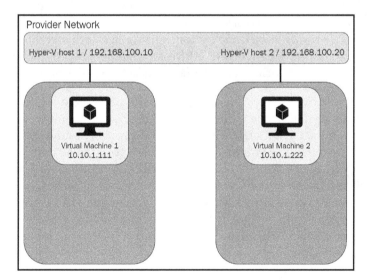

Virtual Machine 1 is hosted on **Hyper-V host 1** and **Virtual Machine 2** is hosted on **Hyper-V host 2**. If **Virtual Machine 1** wants to send a packet to **Virtual Machine 2**, NVGRE will encapsulate the packet and define PA 1 as a source IP address and PA 2 as a destination IP address. The packet will be sent over the physical network between the two Hyper-V hosts and passed to the destination virtual machine on **Hyper-V host 2**. In this scenario, you can configure virtual machines with the same IP addresses on the same or on different Hyper-V hosts. The GRE header includes a **Key** field, which represents a virtual subnet ID. In network virtualization implementation, you need to define a virtual subnet ID to each virtual network that is used by a virtual machine.

Network virtualization policies

Although GRE knows how to encapsulate packets in order to establish communication between two virtual machines on two different Hyper-V hosts, the Hyper-V hosts need to know where the destination virtual machines are located before GRE performs the encapsulation process. If both virtual machines are on the same Hyper-V host, that is not a problem, because Hyper-V already has the necessary information. Because you cannot rely on this scenario, however, as virtual machines are usually hosted on more than two Hyper-V hosts, you need to configure network virtualization to ensure that the virtual machines can communicate. This needs to be done by configuring network virtualization policies. These policies define mapping between IP addresses that are used by virtual machines and Hyper-V host IP addresses, in other words, mapping between CA and PA addresses.

Before the traffic is sent over a physical network, the Hyper-V host will check the network virtualization policies to determine which Hyper-V host is the target for the destination virtual machine. Then the packet can be encapsulated properly and delivered to the right virtual machine. For example, if you have two different companies that are hosted in your datacenter and they have the same IP addresses, without properly configured network virtualization policies, packets could be delivered to the wrong virtual machine. To avoid this scenario, you need to configure mappings and include the virtual subnet ID in policies. As mentioned, the virtual subnet ID will be added as the **Key** field during the encapsulation process, which will ensure that the packet is delivered to the correct virtual network and virtual machine.

The following diagram shows the different virtual machines that use the same CA IP addresses in SDN, with different subnet IDs:

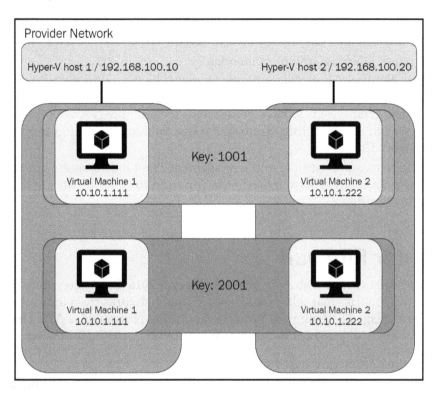

Network Controller

Network Controller is a Windows Server 2016 role that gives you the ability to configure, monitor, manage, and troubleshoot virtual and physical networks in your datacenter, by using two **Application Programming Interfaces** (**APIs**):

- **Southbound API**: This is responsible for communicating with network devices, services, and components. It can also be used to discover network devices, detect configurations, collect information about networks, and send information to the network infrastructure.

- **Northbound API**: This provides the ability to collect network information from Network Controller. This API enables you to configure, monitor, troubleshoot, and deploy new devices on the network by using PowerShell, a REST API, Virtual Machine Manager, or Operations Manager.

Network Controller can be deployed on more than one machine. Although it is a Windows Server 2016 role, Network Controller has some requirements:

- It can only be deployed to the Windows Server 2016 Datacenter edition.
- The management client must be installed on Windows 8 or later.
- Dynamic DNS registration is mandatory.
- If the Network Controller and management client machines are domain-joined machines or virtual machines, you need to create two security groups. The first security group needs to have permissions to configure Network Controller, while the second security group needs to have permissions to configure and manage Network Controller.
- If the Network Controller and management client machines are not domain-joined machines or virtual machines, you need to create certificate-based authentication.

Datacenter Firewall

Datacenter Firewall is a new feature in Windows Server 2016 that helps you to install and configure firewall policies that will protect your virtual networks from unwanted traffic. Its policies can be managed by using the Network Controller Northbound API. The benefits that Datacenter Firewall provides to cloud service providers are the following:

- Provides a software-based firewall solution
- Allows you to easily move tenant virtual machines to different compute hosts without firewall issues
- Provides protection for tenant virtual machines

There are also benefits that are important to tenants:

- It defines internet-facing firewall rules.
- It defines firewall rules to protect traffic between the same or different L2 virtual networks.
- It defines firewall rules to isolate traffic between the tenant virtual network and the on-premise network.

Software Load Balancing

Windows Server 2016 gives you the ability to use SLB in SDN to distribute traffic between available network resources. SLB provides the following features:

- Layer 4 load-balancing for TCP or UDP traffic
- Public and internal network traffic load-balancing
- Support for dynamic IP addresses on VLANs
- Support for health probes

The SLB infrastructure consists of the following components:

- **A Virtual Machine Manager**: This is used to configure Network Controller, the Health Probe, and the SLB Manager.
- **Network Controller**: This role is needed to configure SLB. The network controller will process the SLB commands, calculate the policy for distribution, and provide a health status and MUX.
- **SLB MUX**: This is responsible for rewriting internet traffic and delivering it to dynamic IP. MUX holds the VIP, uses BGP to advertise VIPs to the router, and can consist of one or more machines.
- **Hosts that run Hyper-V**: SLB can only be configured on Windows Server 2016 where the Hyper-V role is already installed.
- **SLB Host Agent**: This listens for SLB policy updates.
- **SDN-enabled Hyper-V Virtual Switch**

Summary

In this chapter, we have learned how to implement high-performance network features in Windows Server 2016. We have also learned about SDN and the most important components of an SDN network. This chapter covered the various SDN components, such as Network Controller, Datacenter Firewall, and SLB.

In the next chapter, we will cover the infrastructure of Active Directory. We will discuss why we need AD DS, what the components of AD DS are, how to install and configure AD DS, and how to create and manage AD DS objects.

Questions

1. How many network adapters can be used in NIC Teaming?
    1. **Up to 32**
    2. Up to 16
    3. Up to 24
    4. Up to 8

2. How many network adapters can be used in SET?
    1. Up to 32
    2. Up to 16
    3. Up to 24
    4. **Up to 8**

3. What is the lowest Windows Server edition in which you can deploy Network Controller?
    1. Windows Server 2016 Standard
    2. Windows Server 2012 Datacenter
    3. Windows Server 2012 Standard
    4. **Windows Server 2016 Datacenter**

4. Which type of IP address is assigned to a virtual machine in an SDN scenario?
    1. **CA**
    2. PA
    3. AA
    4. IP

5. Which two APIs are part of Network Controller?
    1. **South-bound API**
    2. East-bound API
    3. **North-bound API**
    4. West-bound API

6. Which type of IP address is assigned to the Hyper-V host in an SDN scenario?
    1. CA
    2. IP
    3. AC
    4. **PA**

7. What is the latest version of SMB?
   1. SMB 2.x
   2. SMB 3.0.1.
   3. SMB 4
   4. SMB 3.1.1.

8. Are SMB Direct and SMB Multichannel enabled by default on Windows Server 2016?
   1. **Yes**
   2. No

Further reading

For further reading, you can use the following links:

- https://docs.microsoft.com/en-us/windows-server/networking/sdn/plan/plan-a-software-defined-network-infrastructure.
- https://docs.microsoft.com/en-us/previous-versions/orphan-topics/ws.11/mt210892(v=ws.11).
- https://docs.microsoft.com/en-us/windows-server/networking/sdn/technologies/network-function-virtualization/software-load-balancing-for-sdn.
- https://docs.microsoft.com/en-us/windows-server/networking/sdn/technologies/network-function-virtualization/datacenter-firewall-overview.
- https://docs.microsoft.com/en-us/windows-server/networking/sdn/technologies/network-controller/network-controller.
- https://docs.microsoft.com/en-us/windows-server/networking/technologies/nic-teaming/nic-teaming.
  https://docs.microsoft.com/en-us/windows-server/networking/sdn/technologies/set-for-sdn.

Another Book You May Enjoy

If you enjoyed this book, you may be interested in the another book by Packt:

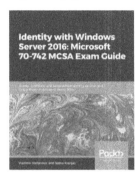

Identity with Windows Server 2016: Microsoft 70-742 MCSA Exam Guide
Vladimir Stefanovic, Sasha Kranjac

ISBN: 978-1-83855-513-9

- Install, configure, and maintain Active Directory Domain Services (AD DS)
- Manage Active Directory Domain Services objects
- Configure and manage Active Directory Certificate Services
- Configure and manage Group Policy
- Design, implement, and configure Active Directory Federation Services
- Implement and configure Active Directory Rights Management Services

Leave a review - let other readers know what you think

Please share your thoughts on this book with others by leaving a review on the site that you bought it from. If you purchased the book from Amazon, please leave us an honest review on this book's Amazon page. This is vital so that other potential readers can see and use your unbiased opinion to make purchasing decisions, we can understand what our customers think about our products, and our authors can see your feedback on the title that they have worked with Packt to create. It will only take a few minutes of your time, but is valuable to other potential customers, our authors, and Packt. Thank you!

Index

www.ingramcontent.com/pod-product-compliance
Lightning Source LLC
Chambersburg PA
CBHW080530060326
40690CB00022B/5082